# Awakening
# to the Power Within

~~R...~~,

Thank-you and Aloha

Mary-Glen Scot

4-20-09

# Awakening
# to the Power Within

◆

## Breaking free from a destructive relationship

*Mary-Glen Scot*

iUniverse, Inc.
New York Lincoln Shanghai

# Awakening to the Power Within
## Breaking free from a destructive relationship

iUniverse books may be ordered through booksellers or by contacting:

iUniverse
2021 Pine Lake Road, Suite 100
Lincoln, NE 68512
www.iuniverse.com
1-800-Authors (1-800-288-4677)


ISBN-13: 978-0-595-33919-8 (pbk)
ISBN-13: 978-0-595-78709-8 (ebk)
ISBN-10: 0-595-33919-0 (pbk)
ISBN-10: 0-595-78709-6 (ebk)

Printed in the United States of America

# Contents

# *Acknowledgment*

*I dedicate this book to God, my Power Greater Than Myself, and to my precious family members—especially my beloved one, Paul.*

*It is also written in honor of my unconditionally loving family members of Alcoholics Anonymous, Al-Anon and Alateen, and all of the volunteer work they do for others. I love each and every one of them in a very special way.*

*To my program sponsees, and to my sponsors, who have helped me grow and become the person I always hoped to be.*

Mary-Glen Scot, 2005

# Twelve Steps

1. We admitted we were powerless over alcohol—that our lives had become unmanageable.

2. Came to believe that a Power greater than ourselves could restore us to sanity.

3. Made a decision to turn our will and our lives over to the care of God *as we understood Him.*

4. Made a searching and fearless moral inventory of ourselves.

5. Admitted to God, to ourselves, and to another human being the exact nature of our wrongs.

6. Were entirely ready to have God remove all these defects of character.

7. Humbly asked Him to remove our shortcomings.

8. Made a list of all persons we had harmed, and became willing to make amends to them all.

9.  Made direct amends to such people wherever possible, except when to do so would injure them or others.

10. Continued to take personal inventory and when we were wrong promptly admitted it.

11. Sought through prayer and meditation to improve our conscious contact with God *as we understood Him,* praying only for His will for us and the power to carry that out.

12. Having had a spiritual awakening as the result of these steps, we tried to carry this message to others, and to practice these principles in all our affairs.

# *Did You Grow Up with a Problem Drinker?*

1. Do you constantly seek approval and affirmation?

2. Do you fail to recognize your accomplishments?

3. Do you fear criticism?

4. Do you overextend yourself?

5. Have you had problems with your own compulsive behavior?

6. Do you have a need for perfection?

7. Are you uneasy when your life is going smoothly, continually anticipating problems?

8. Do you feel more alive in the midst of crisis?

9. Do you still feel responsible for others, as you did for the problem drinker in your life?

10. Do you care for others easily, yet find it difficult to care for yourself?

11. Do you isolate yourself from other people?

12. Do you respond with fear to authority figures and angry people?

13. Do you feel that individuals and society in general are taking advantage of you?

14. Do you have trouble with intimate relationships?

15. Do you confuse pity with love, as you did with the problem drinker?

16. Do you attract and/or seek people who tend to be compulsive and/or abusive?

17. Do you cling to relationships because you are afraid of being alone?

18. Do you often mistrust your own feelings and the feelings expressed by others?

19. Do you find it difficult to identify and express your emotions?

20. Do you think parental drinking may have affected you?

From *Did You Grow Up with a Problem Drinker?* copyright 1984 by Al-Anon Family Group Headquarters, Inc. Reprinted with permission of Al-Anon Family Group Headquarters, Inc.

# *Are You Troubled by Someone's Drinking?*

## Al-Anon is for You!

1. Do you worry about how much someone else drinks?

2. Do you have money problems because of someone else's drinking?

3. Do you tell lies to cover up for someone else's drinking?

4. Do you feel that if the drinker cared about you, he or she would stop drinking to please you?

5. Do you blame the drinker's behavior on his or her companions?

6. Are plans frequently upset or canceled, or meals delayed because of the drinker?

7. Do you make threats such as, "If you don't stop drinking, I'll leave you"?

8. Do you secretly try to smell the drinker's breath?

9. Are you afraid to upset someone for fear it will set off a drinking bout?

10. Have you been hurt or embarrassed by a drinker's behavior?

11. Are holidays and gatherings spoiled because of drinking?

12. Have you considered calling the police for help, in fear of abuse?

13. Do you search for hidden alcohol?

14. Do you ever ride in a car with a driver who has been drinking?

15. Have you refused social invitations out of fear or anxiety?

16. Do you feel like a failure because you can't control the drinking?

17. Do you think that if the drinker stopped drinking, your other problems would be solved?

18. Do you ever threaten to hurt yourself to scare the drinker?

19. Do you feel angry, confused, or depressed most of the time?

20. Do you feel there is no one who understands your problems?

From *Are You Troubled by Someone's Drinking?* copyright 1980 by Al-Anon Family Group Headquarters, Inc. Reprinted with permission of Al-Anon Family Group Headquarters, Inc.

# *Preface*

Welcome. My name is Mary-Glen Scot, and I've been waiting a long time to have the opportunity to greet you and share my experience, strength, and hope with you in a very personal, humble, and honest manner.

The book in your hands is not an autobiography, nor is it intended to be a memoir, and by no means was it written to promote or advertise the Twelve-Step program, of which I am a very happy, grateful, long-time member. We attract only by our example. Rather, it's to share with you some personal solutions I arrived at by working the principles of the Twelve Steps of the Al-Anon Family Groups, Inc., with the help and love of other members. Those solutions ultimately led me to have the serenity my soul had always yearned for. I am humbly hoping it will become a book of inspiration for you also.

If you choose to seek out a Twelve-Step program, I'm sure you will be influenced by the tranquility and collective wisdom of most of those in attendance. If you decide not to do that, I pray that something I've written might lead you in a new spiritual direction and way of living, regardless of what your present age may be.

Are you living an unhappy life right now because of someone else's addictions and/or irresponsible, unacceptable behavior? Then you are one of the many I hope to reach. Do you wish you had peace and harmony in your life today? I hope something I've written will persuade you that it is possible to make a happy life for yourself. Your happiness begins with you, and no one else. When you love and trust your own self, everything else falls entirely into place, for you will learn what you need, when you are ready, and when the time is right for you.

I haven't included any workbook exercise pages. You are a unique person, and I believe you will process your own thoughts and actions with the help of a Divine Power of your own choosing. We must find our own truths within our heart and soul, not that of another—no matter how much we love and adore them. A Power much greater than yourself guides you. We all have one within us; however, you may not have discovered and become *aware* of that Power yet.

Perhaps, if we were face to face in a discussion, you would tell me you are not unhappy because of someone else's addiction problems. I hope you will try to apply some of the principles of a Twelve-Step program to your challenges in daily life, just as an experiment anyway, to see where they will lead you. We will be on a journey of love, contentment, and serenity, together.

Mary-Glen Scot

# *Introduction*

I am writing under the pseudonym of Mary-Glen Scot to protect my anonymity, and possibly that of some others, in accordance with the traditions of my support groups.

I am not a professional writer, and I certainly do not consider myself to be an expert in the Al-Anon Twelve-Step philosophy. We believe that we have no experts or professionals among the average group members in our program. I am a senior citizen who spent most of my life longing for a completely tranquil way of living life on a daily basis. You may think that serenity would be practically impossible to find because of the turmoil, chaos, and terrorism we face in our world today; however, I now believe, after a lifetime of analyzing and questioning the big mystery of life, that external things cannot bring me peace. I can only find that within myself.

I devoted about forty years of my life trying to "cure" an actively drinking alcoholic husband, and that was complete insanity, as we express it in the Second Step of Al-Anon. When I reached my own bottom (as it's described in our program) and felt very despondent, I was directed by the Pastor of my church to an Al-Anon Family Group.

I had never heard of this support group. Even when my husband was in a large treatment center, no one approached me to suggest that I could find my own help in a place called Al-Anon. I may have heard the name Al-Anon off and on, but I always thought it referred to Alcoholics Anonymous, and I was positive I was not addicted to alcohol. I believe the program was just a little *too* anonymous in my earlier years of experiencing another's alcoholism. I was finally convinced that I needed help to find a reason to continue living, to hope for a new way of life; and I did—with the help of those support groups. He chose to continue on his path of destruction, and I was helpless to stop him.

My primary goal was to live a more meaningful life, to feel safe and loved, and that I had a purpose on this earth. I was taught to begin by giving these things to *myself.* My spiritual path in Al-Anon led me to look inward—instead of using survival techniques like trying to control and manipulate others, especially my loved ones. This book is not about how I intellectualized the Twelve Steps, nor do I share about the active alcoholic's "drunkalogs" or my "sobalongs." Rather, it's related to how I worked the program into my life with all of my heart and soul, until it became just second nature, a new way of spiritually enriched living; without my self-will in charge. The Twelve Steps helped me find the inner peace I had been searching for most of my life.

I do not claim to be a representative of, but rather an active member of Al-Anon Family Groups, Inc., and I have been for many years now. My understanding of it is that the Twelve Steps they use are based on two of the oldest spiritual concepts in the world: "I have a Power Greater Than Myself that provides everything I need," and "Love one another." My religion had taught me the phrase love one another; however, I feel that a Twelve-Step program taught me how to go about doing that.

In our meetings, we won't give you advice on how you *should* or *could* live your life, rather we share our experience, strength and hope, and we help others find their own answers from within. I show you my scars and wounds, and how contented and happy I am now. The best evidence that the Twelve-Step principles bring peace and contentment to one's life *is by the example of many members.*

You may have heard of Twelve-Step recovery support groups and wondered what they represent. The Twelve Steps are a spiritual process, not affiliated with any particular religion, treatment center, or political entity. Their members are free to choose a Higher Power that is uniquely their own. In this book, when I speak of my faith in that Higher Power, I use the expressions: "God *of my understanding*," a "Power Greater Than Myself," "Higher Power," or "my God," for the reason that these are phrases commonly used in a Twelve-Step program process. I have many other beautiful adjectives and names I use to describe my God, but they are from my religion, and we do not use any religious tenets in our support meetings; therefore, I do not use them in my writing.

I have been a member of a Twelve-Step group for many years, and I've made a commitment to weave the spiritual principles of the Steps into my daily actions in all of my relationships. We refer to studying and putting them into action in our lives as: "working my program." We, the members of such groups, are created with individual talents and personalities, and we use these to work the Steps in a manner that is as unique as our individual set of fingerprints. The proof that the Twelve Steps can work to bring peace and harmony into one's life is proven by the experience of many Twelve-Step members throughout the world. Without others in the program, I am not enough; I need others to help me; I need others so I can help them.

The effort to use the Steps in my daily life brought me to the realization that my key to hope for serenity was by developing faith in a Power that is above and beyond anything I could ever imagine. Without owning the belief that this Divine Power flows from my God, I could not work the spiritual process of the Twelve Steps. I had to establish a strong relationship in the first three Steps with God before I could make any further progress.

The enlightenment I received from my Higher Power, as well as from other program members, led me to enjoy life to its fullest, and not simply exist. I changed myself only in this process because I am powerless over all others, especially the actively drinking alcoholic that caused me to finally seek the help I desperately needed. As a woman and mother, I always felt that I had to be the one who kept the family happy, well-fed, nurtured, feeling safe, and comforted. Before this century, most history books have depicted women as playing a servant role. I daily thank God for giving me the gift of the opportunity to work the Twelve Steps into my life, and for guiding me to a much better place by changing those old beliefs.

With all of the healing I accomplished in the Steps, I was able to accept my wounds and the part I had played in my unhappiness with my first husband. I also awakened from the denial of my own true self. I had a long, troubled journey before finding Al-Anon, but with the help of other members I found hope and enthusiasm for the future. I could begin having happy dreams and goals again.

I live a very comfortable, serene life now, with the help of God and my support groups. I've made a solemn vow that I will never again let anyone or anything take away my dignity, self-respect, and self-worth that I have earned through a lot of effort and dedication to my program. With prayer and meditation daily, God provides the wisdom, the program tools, and a Power that never fails, and the rest is up to me. I no longer dwell in the negative memories of the past—the pain and sadness of living with the active disease of alcoholism. I only recall, when I feel a need to do so, all of the happy times, and the memories of love that we shared between us and with our precious daughters. There is joy and love in those memories, and kindness and compassion for the way we were.

A program mentor told me, "When God gives you a vision, Mary, act on it, because with time it will fade." With His help, I have faith that He has given me the motivation to write this, so that you may also find hope, harmony, and inner peace—known in our program as serenity—and then you may wish to pass it on to others. The Twelve-Step program works for me in this manner, and I'm positive it also will in your life; if you have the willingness to try it.

At present there are more than one hundred different types of Twelve-Step family support programs listed on the Internet, and I am sure you will find one that will fit your needs and give you hope for a better life in the immediate future.

I am firmly convinced that I, myself, am one of our Twelve-Step program's miracles, and now I will proceed to tell you why.

Mary-Glen Scot

# PART I

## My Life Before Working

## the Twelve Steps

# 1

## *My Childhood in Scotland*

I was born in Glasgow, Scotland, and I lived there until I was sixteen. I am a descendent of the infamous Rob Roy MacGregor of Scotland, and the MacGregor Clan is a very proud, strong, group of people with a lot of courage. You may remember a movie made about Rob Roy a few years ago; it was a little too much "blood and guts" for me. My grandmother's name was Mary-Glen MacGregor, and I was given her full name as my first name, in her honor. (Rob Roy's wife was also named Mary.) Before my program, I perceived their pride as arrogance, and I didn't want to be a participant in any part of that; however, I can now see my perception of them as having been influenced by my own low self-esteem, ingrained in me because of verbal abuse in childhood. Today, I am very proud to proclaim myself a part of the great MacGregor Clan, and I use my whole first name frequently.

I was an only child, and I had a physically and verbally abusive mother. She was the second of twelve children in her family, and had convinced herself that she never wanted to have any of her own! She had experienced enough child raising, and told me so over and over again. She was a very hostile lady to everyone, and I was left feeling all of my life (until now) that I was entirely unwanted and unnecessary. She used to tell me that I was the cause of all of her illness, and she'd rattle off a list of diseases, which as a hypochondriac she thought she had. She loved to tell me dreadful tales of how many hours she was in labor in childbirth with me and how much agony she suffered. I was a breech birth, as she called it. I think that that meant that I was born doubled in two; I am sure it was painful, but that was not my fault. I am afraid she thought so, or at least she tried to make me think so for the rest of my life.

She constantly informed me, when I was a child, that she was not going to live much longer, and that I would have to "take good care of my father when she was gone." I really believed her, and I remember constantly worrying about her impending death; however, the gift from that turned out to be that I did learn to be a good cook and housekeeper at a very young age, and became very independent as far as taking care of my own needs. She convinced everyone that she had a "weak" heart; nevertheless, she lived until she was eighty-seven and died of a heart attack; about seventeen years after the death of my father, whom I adored.

Looking back at my childhood, I'm sure I felt I had no choices, and no human being I could trust enough to confide in with my problems. I couldn't tell anyone at all about my problems with her, for fear she would be even angrier with me, so the best way to escape reality was to dream of the possibility of a better tomorrow. As a result, I lived in fantasy, and not the reality of what I was actually facing each day. I think that was my mental escape—my emotional runaway. I was extremely shy and introverted as a child, and always had my head buried in a book. I loved to read, and I lived in a fantasy world with all of the delightful characters in the children's stories I brought home by armloads from the library. I had a lot of imaginary friends, and I still remember some of those childhood stories almost word for word. I'm sure God helped me cope with the lack of love and caring from my mother by doing that.

My parents gave me the impression that they were agnostics and never had a desire to belong to a church; however, I had a great-grandmother who made sure that I was baptized and attended Sunday school, beginning when I was three years old. My first religious experience was a little non-denominational church named "Paddy Black's Mission." They taught me that I had a very loving, caring, heavenly Father and to trust that He would provide for me.

Above all, I remember the hymns about the love of God for all of us Occasionally, we'd go on a Sunday school picnic to a nearby park and I would be accompanied by my mother's sisters and brothers, a few of whom were about my age. We were transported there on the back of a large flatbed trailer on wheels (we called it a lorry in those days), pulled by beautiful Clydesdale horses. To this day, I am very fond of my relatives. Some are dead now, but the rest still reside in and around the town of Stirling—the same area where the Clan MacGregor has been since the recorded history of Scotland began.

That street in Glasgow where I was born is now full of automobiles; the tenements are all gone, having been replaced by modern apartment-style buildings. The descendents of the Clydesdale horses in Glasgow (on the river Clyde) are only shown worldwide on special occasions now. I've read that during the process of tearing down the old buildings in part of Glasgow, the authorities discovered old dungeons underneath them where people used to be imprisoned when they would steal something, or be accused of other crimes, hundreds of years ago. Of course, I don't know how true that is, part of it is hearsay, but I tend to believe it. The City of Glasgow in Scotland has extremely ancient roots.

This tenement life of mine ended when, during World War Two, the German Air Force bombed the Clydebank area of Glasgow (the largest shipbuilding area in the world at that time). Their mission was to destroy the shipyards, but they also leveled many tenements nearby, and many innocent people died. I remember going through town on the tramcar after a bombing, and hearing my mother sob when we passed a totally destroyed tenement building where a lifetime friend had once lived.

To save the future population of Scotland, the government decided to evacuate all the children whose parents were willing to have them live in Canada for the duration of the war. My parents were going to let me do that, but at the last minute they could not stand to let me leave them. The ship I had been scheduled to sail on was torpedoed as it attempted to cross the Atlantic Ocean in the fall of 1939, and about three hundred children died. That was a tragedy, but it seems that God had other plans for my life.

In a further effort to save future generations, in 1939 the city of Glasgow (a large city, even then) proceeded to evacuate all the children of parents who were willing to send them out into the nearby less populated farming countryside. My mother volunteered to be one of the adults to accompany the children and supervise their welfare since she wanted to be with me. (Its possible she wanted to do that for her own safety, also, but I'll give her the benefit of the doubt on that one.)

We moved to Eaglesham, a small village only about twelve miles from Glasgow, but it was far enough removed from the bombing of the Clydebank to provide a feeling of safety. Each child was given a full grocery bag of food to carry with them, and I think it's easy for me to recall that because it had a delicious Cadbury's chocolate bar in it!

I adored my father; however, during the duration of World War II, I only saw him briefly on Sunday as he worked overtime seven days per week in defense work at the Rolls Royce factory in Glasgow. He told me years later, after I was married, that he never knew of any problem I had with my mother. I tend to believe him, because I was afraid to tell him anything about my mother—afraid that he would also turn against me.

In that era, in elementary school, we daily practiced wearing our gas masks. As children, we thought they were hysterical and that we looked like Mickey Mouse with them on, so they offered no hint of possible danger to us. Thank God, Hitler never did use gas chemicals as a mass weapon during WW II against Britain, for the reason that most of the masks fit too loosely on the children to be of any help against it.

My mother and I found a little two-room, whitewashed cottage for rent in a hamlet called Millhall, about two miles from the village. There was a dam built across the river, and a granary mill was in full operation at that time, with about a half a dozen cottages clustered around it. I've been told that the cottage we lived in is now part of a national historic preserved site. My little wire-haired terrier used to prowl around the mill and kill the rats, and the owner of the mill loved him. Wire-haired terriers were bred for that purpose at one time. I am happy he never acquired the habit of bringing dead ones home to proudly show us his trophies, as a cat would have done. (I can still cry over any dead animals.)

The cottages we lived in were all part of a dairy and potato-growing farm, and had been built for the mill and farm workers. I became a country girl for about six years, and I loved it. Those were some of the happiest years of my life, in spite of having lots of emotional problems, which stemmed from living with my mother. I lived in constant fear of her violent rages. I enjoyed the little country school in Eaglesham; however, I lived two miles from the main village and my friends at school were too far away to play and interact with. Consequently, I had few companions my age.

To escape my mother's bizarre personality I used to take my little dog "Pal" and walk for miles, when the weather permitted. The old river meandered around the homes and farms, and there was a natural abundance of fragrant bluebells, huge foxgloves, primroses, wild hyacinths, Dutch iris, and beautiful ferns. I'm positive now that is where I learned to appreciate the beauty of nature, and there was absolutely no doubt in my mind that God created all of that beauty.

I was alone a lot, but I don't remember feeling lonely because I had a vivid imagination and used to speak to make-believe playmates. I also had interesting conversations with God a lot, and He seemed to give me great answers. He was my heavenly Father that lived away up there somewhere in that vast amount of sky, and He was my confidant for any problems that I brought to Him. Mainly, I remember feeling His presence, and He gave me the comfort and love I felt I did not receive from my mother.

I don't recall receiving any love from my schoolteachers, either, because during that time in Scotland the Headmaster (school principal) would take a heavy leather strap to our hands if we were a few minutes late. The teachers would curl up their leather strap and throw it over to our desk if they thought we were daydreaming. They would then ask us a question, and if we couldn't come up with the correct answer, they would have us bring the strap up to him/her and "let us have it" across our hands with all of their strength in front of our classmates. Those were the "good old days?" I don't think so…However, only one experience with that leather beating on the hands did make me keep my mind on what any teacher was saying from that moment on. I learned from my mistakes early in life.

I moved to Los Angeles in 1948 with my parents, after World War II. Actually, we were originally destined for Pretoria, South Africa, where my father had been offered an excellent job. His goal was to come to the United States, but the passenger liners were booked solid for years to the U.S., so he accepted the job in South Africa. Unexpectedly, shortly after receiving verification of his being hired in South Africa, the United States Lines notified us that they had cancellations immediately on a ship to New York. My parents changed their plans, sold everything in about two weeks; and we were on our way!

We came here without a sponsor because the American consul in Glasgow felt my father and mother had enough money saved that they would not be a burden to anyone. (They had been misers all during World War II and had hoarded quite a small fortune.) We were detained temporarily, and came close to being held permanently on Ellis Island, due to the fact that they thought that no one had ever come to the U.S. without being sponsored by someone guaranteeing responsibility for his or her welfare. The authorities finally allowed us to enter New York and we stayed there for about a week while my parents' money was transferred to the U.S. I remember being very enthralled with all of the bright lights on Broadway; we had suffered years of blackout measures in Glasgow.

We stayed in Detroit for many weeks, and my father and I both found good jobs, but my mother convinced my father that we should move on to California where it was a warm climate. She reminded him that the only reason she had agreed to move to the United States was to get away from the constant rain and dampness in Scotland. Soon we boarded a train, "The Scout" that took at least four days to cross the United States.

We decided our destination would be San Diego, but when we reached Los Angeles and my mother saw the gorgeous blue skies, orange groves, and no snow or rain, she decided we had gone far enough. Our trunk and baggage went merrily on to their assigned final destination of San Diego and we departed from "The Scout" at the Los Angeles Railroad Station. Shortly thereafter, we were able to retrieve our belongings from the railroad authorities, and we settled permanently in Los Angeles.

I had reluctantly left my grandmother, relatives, and my teenage friends behind me in Glasgow. Consequently, I became very lonely, homesick, and unhappy when I settled here. I went from one denomination of church to another in Los Angeles, searching for a way to have a meaningful relationship with God that would replace my innocent, childlike, complete acceptance of Him. Even without the benefit of having been raised by parents who didn't belong to a church, I had come to depend on Him so much to guide me and love me.

Unfortunately, as a young adult trying to adjust to the very different United States way of life, I felt the world closing in on me and pulling me away from God. All of the emphasis, I felt at that time, was on making money and accumulating material things. No matter what church I went to, I couldn't feel as close to God as I had when I was a child in the countryside of Scotland. He was still there for me, but I was the one who had wandered away from Him.

# 2

# *Becoming Enmeshed in Another's Addiction*

A young Scotsman came into my life in Los Angeles when I was eighteen. He was handsome, well groomed, earned a decent salary, and we were married about eight months later. Both of his parents had died when he was about twelve, and he also had moved here from Glasgow to live with an aunt. He, I thought, would rescue me from my unhappy home life and we'd live happily ever after. I should have known he was an alcoholic when he stopped to buy a pint of Scotch the night we were married, but then fifty years ago we didn't know much about alcoholism—they were just considered "heavy boozers" in those days. My parents had never had a problem abusing alcohol, so I didn't realize what lay ahead for me.

Six weeks after we were married he was drafted and spent two years overseas in the army during the Korean War. He was not yet a United States citizen, but he chose to allow himself to be inducted into the U.S. Army. During those two years I was able to break the chain of control from my mother, and I became very self-sufficient and mature. Unfortunately, he did not, and he spent most of those two years drinking and gambling away his allowance with army buddies. That was the beginning of a lifetime of active alcoholism that drastically affected us both.

All I wanted for my life at that time was to be a homemaker and take care of our two precious babies. Regretfully, I never had the opportunity to do that. I remember that I had a lot of criticism aimed at me because I was a working mother in the 1950s; however, I needed to work outside the home to supplement our income so we could afford a small, old, modest two-bedroom home of our own, instead of a one-bedroom apartment. We had an old car we paid $100 for and when it died, we bought another one! We had no debts other than the house, and we did the best we could for our young age and income. I was positive I must continue to work when I saw the results of other young couples where the wife did not work. They lived in an apartment, had one car, so she was confined to that apartment for many years while her young husband struggled to support them. I didn't want that to happen to us.

I think I became a phony personality when I lived with active alcoholism. I lived in self-denial and insecurity. Actually, now that I think of it, I never gave myself much thought at all. I put a big smile on for the world to see and made believe that I had a loving, caring relationship with my husband. (I guess I followed the advice in the old saying: "Smile and the world smiles with you; weep and you'll weep alone.")

Somewhere along the way, I lost touch with the real me, myself, and I, and I had no self-identity. I put on a big act and created this great image of my husband, as I wanted to portray him. Part of that image was true, but the rest was simply fantasy. I was escaping reality, the way we really lived, and I didn't want anyone to know the truth—how unhappy I actually felt. I was employed in a job where others said they were in a happy, *perfect* relationship with someone, and I believed them. I wanted to be like them, but I felt I had no hope of that because of his bad temper.

When I married at eighteen, I had many wants and needs. Those became my dreams and goals: a lovely home, children, and a husband I could live with forever and be happy with. And I did have all of those dreams and goals fulfilled, except the live-happily-ever-after part. He was a good provider, and we always had a comfortable home in a great middle-class neighborhood for our children. When he caused unhappiness in our lives with his drinking and gambling (which was often), he'd say, "I'm sorry, and I'll buy you something." And I settled for that; I always had wants for something or other. I had endless wants and needs because I tried to make material things substitute for the love, caring, and understanding I felt was lacking in our marriage.

Retail therapy was one of my many ways of escaping reality. I believed that as long as everything was beautiful on the outside, with material things, then I'd be okay. I call that my *fantasy vs. reality* world that I had created, beginning in childhood with an abusive mother; however, that imaginary world failed to bring me the peace and harmony I longed for. That dream world I had fabricated in my mind—an unreal, romantic, idealistic version—only produced emptiness in my heart and soul that couldn't be satisfied with material things created by man.

I kept trying to find ways to help him be happier with his life; I probably thought if he were only happier with himself, then I'd be happy, too. I never gave myself permission in that marriage to satisfy the yearnings of my own soul because of my obsession with what was *going on with him*. Denial protected me from the pain of living with him, but it also rendered me blind to my own feelings, needs, and myself in general.

I kept forgiving him, over and over. I had always been taught in my religion to "turn the other cheek." Looking back, did I really forgive him, or did I just deceive myself? Wasn't it based on the fear that I wouldn't be able to survive on my own? That was probably true, and I felt I had no choice but to stay with him. In the process, I lost all of my own self-respect and dignity, just as I had done as a child with my mother.

I was against divorce, and I felt my marriage vows were not just a commitment to him, but to God also, and I wanted to make the marriage work. I was extremely depressed and unhappy, and I felt trapped in the marriage. I couldn't understand at that time that I had choices I could make for myself of whether or not to continue living with him. I felt I was a victim, but instead I was a volunteer to his verbal abuse and bad temper. I had condemned myself to a virtual prison of my own making.

I felt I had nowhere to run if I left him. I didn't make enough salary to support the girls and myself in a satisfactory manner; therefore, I felt I had no option other than to stay with him. He always told me he would leave and I'd never find him, and that I would never get any financial aid from him if I filed for a divorce. He often told me, "I'm not leaving; there's the door," and he would push me toward it. I knew I couldn't expect any help at all from my parents financially, or for shelter. My husband's family had enough problems of their own, so I felt hopelessly and helplessly alone with my problem.

I learned, from sad experience, that active alcoholism *is* a progressive debilitating disease. In the beginning we had a happy life together—most of the time, anyway. As the years went on, the percentage of happiness drastically plunged, and I became desperately unhappy with our married life. The shame of having to be seen in public with someone, whose behavior was completely intolerable to me when he was drunk, kept increasing to the point that I found it difficult to socialize as a couple.

In my late thirties, with my father's help, I finally decided to see a lawyer about a divorce. My father was very intuitive and told me, "I'd rather live in a shack than live the way you are doing." When I went to his lawyer, she asked me how much we had in savings accounts, and when I told her about

$2,000—although we did not believe in charge accounts, so we had no debts—she shook her head. (At that point, I think she was no longer interested in my case!) He was also a compulsive gambler (horse racing), and we had never saved extra money. Whatever was left, I used to purchase material goods. We had a nice home and fairly decent cars, but that was it. There was not even enough extra money to file for a divorce…

I changed my mind (one more time) about divorcing him, and let him convince me he would change and we could be happy.

# 3

# *A Dream with a Sad Ending*

Once again, he had covertly manipulated me into thinking that he could change and we would be happy; active alcoholics are expert at that maneuver. So, once again, I proceeded to come up with another one of Mary-Glen's great plans and dreams for our future.

I have always lived in the large, metropolitan area of a city; except for the six years of happiness I experienced as a child in the Scottish countryside. Due to having a great passion for nature and the outdoors, I had a constant longing to live in a rural area, but the only job we had available to either one of us was only to be found in a large city. After our children had finished college and were on their own, I thought it would help our relationship problems if we bought five acres of land in the High Desert, about a hundred miles from the large city, and started building a home for our future retirement. (I was always trying to live way ahead of the here and now.) I thought, in that way, we could have a weekend get-away from the busy city.

To have the money we needed, we refinanced the home we were living in and found our perfect dreamland. We both had happy anticipation of living there some day. For a long time, working on that dream compensated me for what I felt was lacking in my marriage: namely, a gentle, caring companion. I did find most of the peace and tranquility I had been longing for (except for the challenge of the ongoing progressive disease of alcoholism). For the next twenty years, we spent every weekend, as well as our yearly vacations, working on the house. We hired a local contractor to build the outside of the house (the shell), and were able to do the work of the entire inside ourselves. We directed most of our energy and love toward making that home comfortable.

The house sat on top of a knoll in that lovely mountain valley, and we had a panoramic view of many mountain ranges from every window. In the evening, at 5,000 feet elevation, the stars lit up the whole area around the house with their brilliance, and they seemed to be almost within arm's reach. There were no city lights or smog to obscure the view. The air we breathed had a fresh, sweet fragrance that only God could create—especially after a shower of rain. I am sure you can relate to that experience if you have ever lived in a smoggy city and escaped it by temporarily going to a higher rural elevation.

We cleared the wild brush from about an acre of land around the house and planted dozens of fragrant rose bushes, bearded Iris, and left lots of natural wild flowers to grow in all of their glory. I wanted to recreate a replica of the scene in the movie *Dr. Zhivago,* where the spring breaks through the snow, and suddenly a brilliant yellow carpet of a million daffodils appear. People kept donating their extra daffodil bulbs, and I don't know how many we ended up with—they just kept multiplying. They were the only bulbs the ground squirrels wouldn't dig up and eat!

My good memories during that marriage, apart from our two wonderful daughters, are the years that we spent at that house with the five acres in the high desert in Southern California. The skies were a brilliant blue, and we had glorious sunshine, unlike Scotland with its damp climate. The closest small city was about fifty miles away, and we were out of reach of the smog and the heavy traffic in the Los Angeles/Orange County area. I had always longed to live in the countryside again and grow flowers and vegetables, but I didn't have enough space in the city garden to do that, so having five acres was like having a paradise on earth for me.

We planted over a hundred fruit and shade trees. It was the 1970s when the *back to the land* movement began, and we were going to produce all of our own necessities of living—or at least I had it planned that way. I felt I would be helping our family survive the coming disastrous economic crash that was predicted by many financial experts at that time, if we could be self-sufficient and grow most of our own food. (There was a severe economic recession for many years, and my husband temporarily was unemployed, but by God's Grace we recovered and were financially okay.)

I happily spent many hours a day planting those trees in my spare time; and I prayed for each one of them as I planted it. They all flourished, in spite of the tornado-like winds and the gophers that plagued that valley. I loved every single one of those beautiful trees. I read *Mother Earth* magazines endlessly to try to learn how to live on our own resources. In retrospect, that was merely another one of my romantic, idealistic approaches to a way of life that may not even be attainable for the average person, at least as things are today in the United States.

During the forty years I lived in Southern California, quite a few major earthquakes hit the area. I am terrified of earthquakes and that may go back to my experiences of seeing the effects of large tenements lying in rubble as a child in WW II. I do trust my God to get me safely through them—I just don't like the experience while it's happening!

Not too long after we finished successfully having a well drilled and completed the house, we discovered that teams of geologists were running tests on the earthquake fault that ran through the valley. An article appeared in a popular national magazine about their findings, and they said their results indicated that an earthquake of a high magnitude was imminent in the near future on that fault. Further, they stated that it was the most active fault in California. *We later realized that we had inadvertently built our new home near the top of the path of that fault.* I was devastated to find that out, but many months later we decided we would keep the house anyway, give our concerns about it to God, and trust that everything would be okay.

Little did I know that twenty years down the road I would be facing something perhaps more destructive than that predicted earthquake—that alcoholism would destroy our love and lives together. Today I know that alcoholism damages many others apart from the alcoholic himself. (That earthquake in that beautiful valley has yet to materialize. We had one about 4.0 on the Richter scale while we owned the property, but it did no damage.)

The twenty years when we had our part-time home, I did not attend any church, but I kept my faith in God, and I loved living in that rural setting. The atmosphere in that valley was heavenly for me, but my husband used it as an opportunity and excuse for more drinking. The closest highway patrol office was fifty miles away, and he could drive on the rural roads with nary a care. Some of the local people did drive without any fear of reprisal—or a driver's license and insurance for that matter. They felt they were "safe" from the law if they kept to the rural dirt roads.

As years went by, I became the wife of a drunk, and I had to socialize with friends of his choosing, who were also, of course, drunks. Most actively drinking alcoholics are not emotionally healthy, happy people to begin with, and most of them drink excessively to kill their bad opinions of themselves. I couldn't cultivate friendships with spiritually thinking people, as he was not comfortable around that type of personality. That led me to resist any self-expression of my own heart and soul, since I felt his friends would think I was being self-righteous and prudish if I didn't join in the drinking and off-color jokes. That denial of my true inner self was people-pleasing behavior in those days. I always felt that I did not fit in with his choice of acquaintances, and I had few friends of my own.

I later gave up drinking wine in the evening except on special family celebrations. I felt I never had a serious problem with drinking, anyway. Some people, even some friends and family (especially the alcoholics) did not like that at all. Perhaps they thought it was a threat to them, but I felt I should not continue to use something that had only brought pain into my life.

My husband's disease progressively got worse as the years went on, and I finally convinced him to sell our special country property. Because of the active alcoholism, I could see no future happiness living there alone with him. I remember him saying, "I can't believe you're making me do this." I still have some guilt about that, but I realize now that we could not have kept up with the work as we approached our seventies. I feel it wasn't a part of God's permanent plan, for me at least, but I still pray for the beautiful trees. Some of them had a special significance for me, for the reason I had first planted them as seedlings in small pots until they grew big enough to survive in that harsh climate. We placed chicken wire around the roots so the gophers wouldn't get them, wire mesh around the trunks so rabbits wouldn't eat them; and, of course, God, creator of heaven and earth, took care of them and helped them grow. The gift from all of that labor, I realize now, was that it kept my mind focused on gardening—not on his unacceptable behavior.

That little village we lived in part-time reminded me of my favorite story of *Brigadoon,* the legendary little mythical village of Scotland, which only comes alive every one hundred years. Maybe I kept hoping I'd disappear off into eternity, just as the people in Brigadoon did in that legend, and never have to face city life again. I heard someone describe eternity one time as "a world where there is time enough and room enough to do all of the things we always wanted to do." (Sure sounds like Brigadoon to me.)

It's strange, all of my life I had been yearning to live in a quieter place, yet I always seemed to end up living in a big city (as I do now); however, I now realize that is where most of us usually find employment. Living in a large metropolitan area does have its advantages; as a senior now, for me that would represent the public libraries, medical facilities, stores, and so forth.

I had dreamed of how wonderful it would be to live in that home permanently on a fulltime basis some day, but that day never came. The disease of active alcoholism shattered any chance of fulfillment of those dreams that we worked so intensively on and in which we tied up all of our life savings. Perhaps I was being selfish, but I'm sure now that I convinced him to sell it for my protection, rather than face a future living there alone with him; with no hope of his seeking sobriety. We were forced to sell it at a loss, after twenty years of labor and love on it, because we found out that most people prefer to buy bare land in an outlying area so they also can build their own dream house. I did help start a fruit orchard with over a hundred trees in that little community and I pray today that the trees have survived; however, I have never had the heart to go back to look at them. I feel now that doing so would cause a great sorrow to arise in my soul.

I had it all so carefully planned. We would retire at fifty-five because we had the land and house paid for. Except, darn it, I didn't know that the disease of alcoholism is a difficult foe to beat, and it is also baffling, cunning, and can destroy everything it comes in contact with if it goes untreated. It destroyed my beautiful fantasy world that I used as an escape from the reality of facing active alcoholism, and I was left feeling hopeless and helpless against it.

In my fellowship, we say "look for the gift in sad experiences." Those experiences led me to have a firm belief in one of the Twelve Step principles: You can plan the plan, but just don't plan the outcome…As my countryman Robert Burns wrote, "The best laid plans of mice and men go often astray—and leave us naught but sorrow for promised joy."

# 4

## *The Last Ten Years of Our Marriage*

He decided not to take an early retirement at fifty-five, and we chose to have one full-time residence only—a smaller home close to our daughters in the big city. One evening I was forced to flee his physically violent threats, and with my son-in-law's help, I took the motor home and went into seclusion in an RV park where he wouldn't be likely to look for me. When I refused to come home, it forced him to admit the need for help, and he agreed to enter an excellent hospital treatment program for about a month or more.

Actually, I was disappointed when he admitted himself for treatment, because I was prepared to live alone by that time. I really hoped that he would peacefully allow me to leave him. He later informed me that he had only gone into treatment because he felt I had forced him to do that, and he did not intend to stay sober. He went back to heavy drinking about a day or two after he left the hospital treatment center where he'd been for six weeks.

I realize now that I should have left him permanently at that point, and I'll never understand why I didn't. Perhaps it was because I was overwhelmed, severely depressed, and just not capable of making a decision for my own best interests. I had such a significant feeling of personal shame and loss of dignity due to having to appear in public at times with a person whose behavior was completely bizarre, so I withdrew more and more inwardly from the reality of the marriage.

He threatened my life a few times, and I never had him charged because I feared a reprisal from him. When I hear other women in dysfunctional relationships speak about trying to kill their husbands, I can't relate to them. I have always been a complete pacifist, and I detest loud voices and arguments; therefore, I avoided confrontations at any cost. My father was also very passive, and my mother felt I had inherited his personality. She saw those actions of mine as behaving in an inferior manner, but I don't agree. Today I can assert myself, but I absolutely have to maintain peace and harmony in my relationships; however, *it's not now at my expense.*

I lived my life before the program as a victim and martyr. When I did allow myself to become friends with another woman, (someone I could talk to about my marriage, which I seldom let myself do), I was given sympathy and attention. Thus I had a valid excuse for not taking responsibility for my own feelings and actions. I can understand now; I became stuck in that unhealthy manner of seeing myself as just an innocent *victim,* and it created a big mucky hole of depression that I didn't know how to pull myself out of.

Undoubtedly, my life was sad as a child and as a young wife living with a compulsive gambler and drinker, but at some point in time I must have had opportunities to turn my circumstances around for the better. Today, with the help of Al-Anon, I can see that somewhere along the way I *should have* recognized that I helped (at least fifty percent of the time) to create part of my unhappiness, *because I didn't make the correct choices for my own benefit.*

I'm quite sure now that I tolerated his alcoholic abusive behavior for so many years for the reason that I felt guilty about the part of the marriage vows "in sickness or health, for better or for worse." That was actually a commitment that I made not only to him, but also to God. I am part of a generation that believed we married only once, even if our "prince" turned into a "frog," and we stayed with that person until we died. A phrase in our marriage vows (at that time, anyway) was, "And the two shall become as one," and we did become as one—enmeshed in the disease of alcoholism. I came to believe, with the help of others in our program, that just as a cancer victim seeks medical help, an alcoholic could also seek help through A.A. to get sober; however, *only if he has the willingness and it's his own desire.*

Sadness welled up in my soul while living with the alcoholism until I could endure it no longer. There's a program saying: "I'll swim with you side by side, but I won't drown with you." I became convinced that I had to break away from him—forever. Little by little, over the years, my love for him was destroyed and the mental abuse was slowly killing me. One evening, after a particularly embarrassing time with him at a large gathering of friends and family, I told my daughter how unhappy I was—for at least the billionth time—and I said, "It will all end with his death or mine." The next day I thought about what I'd said to her and I decided, "No, I don't have to wait for the possibility of it all to end like that."

I made a final decision to leave him. I had lived through broken promises and shattered dreams and goals, and I felt as if my heart had been ripped apart; however, I also felt it was a sin to stay married when we were destroying each other's dignity and self-respect. For us, that eventually led to complete incompatibility. I made a final decision, but I still didn't find the courage to act on it.

Finally, I dreamed up another Mary-my-way great idea to try to find peace in the marriage, but it was just another example of my self-will run riot once again. I was one of the many women with low self-esteem that would go to any lengths to try to save a bad marriage, rather than face the possibility of living alone.

My last big geographic attempt to fill the void in my heart and soul was my dream of escaping reality—once again—in a fully equipped twenty-four-foot motor home. After his failure at sobriety when he left the treatment center, I urged him to take an early retirement at sixty, so we would be free to travel as long as we wished. We both liked traveling in the motor home, and had been doing that on month long vacations from work for many years. I suggested to him that we could travel around the U.S. and Canada and see if we could find a small town with real estate prices compatible with our retirement income. We had lived in California most of our lives, but the real estate prices were going completely sky-high on small homes. I felt if we sold our home in California, we could take the profit from it and live comfortably on our retirement income, and thus be able to afford to continue to travel a lot in the motor home.

I have heard many times that we may travel the world in search of happiness, but our efforts will be futile if we don't take it with us. We traveled eighteen thousand miles in my search for that elusive happiness. He always found fault with small towns in different locations. The realization came to me recently; it was probably because he wanted to be sure the State did not have controlled liquor purchases and that there would also be a way for him to gamble on horse racing. He probably couldn't see retirement without gambling and alcohol. (I could, of course.)

I thought our lives would miraculously change—at least mine would—if we no longer had the responsibility of a house, family, jobs; the usual day-to-day routine. That was simply another way of my denying the reality that we did not have a healthy relationship; however, his alcoholism was progressing in a predictable manner, and that is something I had not accepted and dealt with, or even *expected*. The disease steadily worsens as years accumulate, especially if a practicing alcoholic makes it to retirement, and it did for him. After many years of alcoholic consumption, an alcoholic's body and brain start to rapidly deteriorate.

One of my favorite books to romanticize about when I was younger was Thoreau's *Walden Pond*. Being an incurable romantic idealist, I loved his writing about the joys of self-sufficiency and solitude. We visited that pond while on this long journey and I realized that imagining myself living at Walden Pond, as Thoreau did, was just another fantasy of mine. The reality is, especially as a senior, I need to live in a city with conveniences and not in isolation. Besides which, I have been informed now that Thoreau only lived there for one year—in my eyes now, that is just a long retreat!

Alcohol *rode along* with us on that eighteen-thousand-mile journey, and eight months later I'd seen a lot of awesome scenery and felt much closer to God. However, I suffered through some very painful, emotional and near-death experiences because of his erratic behavior. He didn't drink and drive, but he made sure we arrived at a campground by the middle of the day, and then he would proceed to drink himself into oblivion until the next morning. His justification, of course, was "the stress of driving a motor home for miles." Consequently, I would spend the rest of each day alone, reading or walking along the trails in State parks. I no longer had our beloved Airdale as a companion on walks, so I felt lonely. I certainly had time to do a lot of meditating during those months, and the gift in all of that experience was *I finally woke up and faced reality, instead of mentally running away.*

After many years of active alcoholism, a chasm opened between the two of us—somewhat like a Grand Canyon—that nothing could bridge. I was powerless, but I didn't yet know how to resolve that feeling, because I didn't have Al-Anon to help me with that challenge.

I recall walking along the big desert wash near our home very early every morning before I finally separated from my husband. I loved the native shrubs that grew in abundance there. They have beautiful leaves, like ferns, and lilac-colored blossoms. One day I spotted a seedling of this shrub growing in a small crack between the sidewalk and a block wall. As I walked past it, the thought entered my mind, "It won't survive because of the extreme heat and the concrete around it"; nonetheless, I watched it grow until it became a small, brilliant bush. One morning I looked at it and thought, "If that little seedling can make it in such adverse conditions, with God's help, I will also."

I knew there was more to life than the way we had been living. I know now that my Higher Power did have other ideas and better plans for my future. I call that *God's big plan*—not mine. With the help of my Higher Power and the help of the steps, I began to feel that I could face my future alone with confidence. I had always been afraid that I could not support myself financially, emotionally, and socially if I were on my own. A place well known is a safe place to be, compared to stepping out into the darkness. My darkness was the fear of being alone and financially insecure, and that fear, I'm sure, was a major cause of my staying in that marriage of a lifetime.

On that long motor home trip, my feelings were buried so deeply that I lost any hope I had left that we could live together "happily ever after." When the trip ended, I knew our marriage also must end—for my sake. Being locked up in a motor home with a drunk for such a long time was the final straw. Yet I *still* had trouble finding the courage I needed to face the final battle with alcoholism and leave him.

Instead of going back to California, where we'd lived most of our married life, I suggested we stay a month in the city I call home today. I could never imagine myself living here when we were young, but now, as a senior citizen, I realize it has much to contribute to living a comfortable life, and the price of homes at that time was relatively inexpensive. He wanted to continue living in the motor home, but I needed more room to breathe.

We purchased a home in the city I now live in. It was a lovely home; yet one more time I was looking to material things to make life "all better" for me. Immediately after agreeing to purchase it, I regretted allowing him to convince me to buy it, because my intuition told me I was making a poor decision. But he still tried to convince me that our lives would be better when we lived in a house; and I, once again, allowed him to do that.

Two months later I reached my final bottom, and I knew I had to leave him. I found out that he had gambled our savings slowly away. I had always paid cash for most things in our marriage, so we owed very little on charge accounts. When a collection agency called and got extremely nasty, I found out the sordid truth about what he'd been doing. He had been using the credit card for gambling and tearing up the bills as they arrived, without telling me. I was horrified and told him I wanted a divorce. I have to confess here, that I used the "F" word and called him a "f— idiot." I abhor the "F" word and *never had used it before*, but for the first time ever, he looked at me and said, "I think you mean it; I will help you." Before this turning point, he had threatened me with a gun or a knife if I ever sounded serious about doing that, and I was very grateful to God for helping me. I knew if I did not leave him there would not be enough money left for me to make the move. I had feelings of complete abandonment; nevertheless, I felt I was finally making the best choice for my own welfare.

The morning I reached my bottom, I had asked God to "please help me," just as the alcoholics do. I asked Him to help me end the marriage or take me home with Him. I couldn't have ended much lower than that, could I? That same day that I asked my God for help, I was led by the Pastor of my church to find an Al-Anon meeting.

I had never before sought help. That was, indeed, a profound spiritual awakening—*all because I asked a Power Greater than I am for His help.* Not long afterwards came an overwhelming Spirit filled peace within me that everything was going to be all right in my life. Many times I had prayed to the religious God *of my understanding*, "Thy will be done," but now every day things seemed to be on a totally different acceptance and surrender level; and the result of the action that I, myself, had moved out of my own way. That thought in itself was a new spiritual revelation for me—being able to let God handle life's difficulties. What a wonderful gift I was offered.

In that marriage I had lived for *some day when...*I waited and hoped for happiness that *never came.* I'd put my life on hold for such a long time, and then I woke up to the reality that waiting for *some day when...*doesn't work either, Mary-Glen. Happiness comes from inside yourself, right now, wherever you may be. But you have to work at it.

He refused to leave the home we had just bought until it sold, and instead of forcing him out, I allowed him to have his way. It was about six months before it finally sold, and part of the reason was due to his interference with people viewing the home because of his drunken condition. On one occasion he had blacked out, and before the realtor and clients arrived, I dragged him by his feet into the bedroom and closed the door. I told the realtor he was "sick," and that we couldn't show that room. (Oh, the crazy things we do when we live with the active disease.) Those were some of the worst months of my entire life; however, my Higher Power and my friends in Al-Anon carried me through it all. The people in the meetings slowly helped me feel safe in the belief that God would provide for all of my needs, and He has, and He still does.

It took me more courage and self-trust to leave that marriage than it took to stay in it. Even though I was the one who ended it, I went through a period of mourning that it finally had come to an end, and with it all of my hopes and dreams for the future. When we lose something very precious to our heart and soul, we have to grieve in order to grow from it. But I've learned, and understand—the sad way—I could not appreciate the true joy of living that I now have unless I had experienced emotional sadness, and/or physical pain, at some time in my life. That was one of the gifts in it all.

I did suffer a lot of guilt about leaving him, because with help from others in the program, I had hope for true happiness and serenity in my life, and he didn't. Nevertheless, others helped me realize that I had to keep moving forward with the help of my Higher Power; and that his recovery was not my responsibility. I had to move on alone and give him to God. I also became aware that *I am responsible* for my own level of happiness, *and no relationship can ever completely do that for me.*

I was denied a loving, caring companion for many years, and after our divorce I felt unwanted, unloved, alone and helpless. He threatened me over and over, "You'll never make it on your own." However, with the help of some others, I found a part-time job that only paid $6.00 per hour, but I felt that was sufficient to begin with. He told me, "I wouldn't work for that meager amount," and I responded, "Well, I will, and I'll keep my self-respect and dignity." In the program, I came to believe that my own thinking had to change before I could make a new life for myself, and with God's help, working through others in the support group, I did change for the better.

Other Al-Anons taught me that life's greatest achievement is the continuous remaking of yourself so that, at last, you really know how to live. I believe that in Twelve-Step programs we change and become what we are given; what we are open and willing enough to receive from others in our meetings and put into action in our lives. One day at a time, I changed and became the inner self that they helped me discover. That self was always there, but it had been buried under layers of self-doubt, anger, shame, cynicism, and hopelessness. As I began my journey of self-discovery, I actually began to feel good about myself—I didn't have to feel like a phony personality any longer. It was my life, and I took it back and began a new way of living, with the help of others in my support groups.

# PART II

## Thoughts on the First Nine Steps

# 5

# *Comments on Part II: The First Nine Steps*

There are many books available that offer suggestions on how we might study the Twelve Steps and put them to use in our life and relationships. I'm going to share some of the personal difficulties I experienced in actualizing the steps, in the hope it will lead you to find your own logical understanding of them; however, we strive for spiritual progress—not spiritual perfection. Each one works the Steps at his/her own pace and in his/her own unique way. I'm convinced that only God is perfect; and striving for perfectionism only slows my spiritual growth.

Steps One, Two, and Three, are considered by some to be the "Awareness, Acceptance, and Action" Steps. They are also sometimes thought of as, "I can't, He can, so I'll let Him." Steps Four through Nine are known as the "Healing Steps." Later, in the closing chapters of this book, I'll share my spiritual experiences with Steps Ten, Eleven, and Twelve, known in the program as the "Maintenance Steps."

## The First Three Steps

*"Ask, and it shall be given unto you, seek and you shall find, knock and the door shall be opened." Matthew 7-7*

My understanding of the principles of the first three Steps is this: They are faith; trust in God and myself, and complete honesty about my inner being. My interpretation of faith is to know and understand God, and to develop a strong personal relationship with Him. With the help of a sponsor, I motivated myself to spend the first two years working on those steps, trying to integrate them into my daily pattern of living. I'm aware now that: it took that length of time for the enlightenment about them to happen, and that was caused by the distorted thinking I had developed living with the craziness and chaos of alcoholism. I couldn't make rational decisions for my own emotional health, and I found it necessary to let people in Al-Anon give me their suggestions. Those members became a channel for God's guidance to me. I also needed the first two years to allow healing of old wounds before I could do the difficult job of self-analysis that followed in the Fourth Step.

### Step One: Admitted we were powerless over alcohol—that our lives had become unmanageable.

I asked myself, "Do I have enough power to make myself serene and happy? To find wise solutions to any problems I may have?" The answer was, "Of course not." I had to surrender whatever power I owned over to God. By working on the First Step, the more I admitted how truly powerless I was over other people and circumstances in my life, the more emotionally stronger I became, for the reason that I relied on a Divine Power to guide me. I am still learning that I have a choice between trusting God and struggling by myself. Sometimes a little willingness can work miracles; it has for me.

I had already lost my battle against alcoholism, and I was in despair. I discovered that the strength I was desperately seeking was available to me, mainly through the belief that there is a supernatural being, a force greater than any human power, which will help me, *if I simply ask Him*. At that time I could not actualize that power in my life—that source of comfort, but I could see a Spirit of healing helping others who were in emotional pain. I practiced asking for His help each day by using this prayer: "Please guide me today in all that I say and do," but I hastened to add, "May your will be done only."

I find now that I only have to replace the word "alcohol" in the First Step with whatever the name of the problem is that's confronting me today. The admission of powerlessness—the commitment—can apply to many difficulties I feel I should be able to control, but find out that I cannot. I only have power over my own needs, emotions, actions or reactions, and what I say, think or do. If I exercise that power, problems outside of me will work out without any interference from me.

During my marriage to a husband caught up in the disease I could no more control his behavior than I could control the crazy traffic on my way to work in Orange County. Reflecting now on the way we lived, it also became apparent that my life *had* become unmanageable. I was very often unreasonable, cranky, depressed, and isolated. I devoted all of my time and energy to his problem instead of giving any thought to my own welfare, which was heading inch by inch downhill. In Step One, I became aware of our three "Cs": "I didn't Cause it, can't Cure it, and can't Control it." I slowly began to realize that I had just spent a lifetime trying to fix something that was absolutely beyond my control. People in the fellowship helped me to get the focus back on myself, so I could start living a more rewarding, emotionally healthier life.

With the First Step, I not only accepted and surrendered my powerlessness; *it became an actual commitment and a solemn vow to follow through with it.* Doing that has led me to the idyllic state of having the ability to remain calm and to be able to think logically in the midst of an emotional upheaval involving others and myself. God gives me spiritual solutions if I ask Him. These solutions come to me from various sources: my own inner Spirit, reading our program literature, and what others share in our group meetings.

By truly accepting and believing Step One in my heart, I was able to begin picking up the pieces of my life, and since my life was all that I really could change; it made sense for me to devote my time and energy completely to doing that. By admitting that I was powerless over so many things in this world, I was free to let go of that burden, and I no longer needed to exhaust myself trying to do anything that is humanly impossible.

When I stopped giving others directions, stopped trying to tell them how to run their lives, and followed God's will, I began to experience peace. My sponsor informed me that anything beyond the end of my nose was not my business, and she would point at the tip of her nose if I were talking about anyone else. However, she also taught me that I didn't have to try to live up to someone else's standards and expectations of me. That simple suggestion helped keep the focus on me, and try to change only myself. If that applies to me, then it also works in reverse—about them! What an interesting revelation for someone who always tried to "fix" others and forgot about herself.

Some members suggested that I seek knowledge of a Higher Power's will for those situations and people that I was trying so desperately to control and change. That is what had worked best for them. I didn't want to believe that, and letting go wasn't easy, but guess what? They were right. My life is becoming much more manageable now because I've been taught by their loving example to let go of

"Mary-my-will-be-done." What others say or do is part of their lives. Focusing on my own life means that I am conscious of and accept the reality of a situation. Today I look at my own options, instead of looking at the options that may be available to others.

I used to worry about everything and anything (negative thinking), and in working the First Step with my sponsor; she made me acknowledge that I was powerless over not just alcohol, but all other people, places, and circumstances. I wrote these thoughts while working Step One: "When the light bulb moment finally came and I realized I couldn't do anything at all about my former husband's resentment against me and the world around me (all of the violence in the newspapers and television), I finally accepted and understood powerlessness." My sponsor told me to read this over and over until I got "it": "Self-love will lead to a happier life, where everything just seems to fall into place. Maybe some day I'll look back at all of the hours of work I've done in the Al-Anon process and tell myself, that's what I've been slowly learning all along—the awesome healing power of learning to love myself. That is one power no one can ever take away from me."

Someone asked me recently if I ever get bored or burned out going over the steps repeatedly. I don't, because every time I'm in a Step One group meeting, I try to be like a beginner and keep an open, willing mind. When I do that, I get some new enlightenment of what this Step means to me.

I am very grateful for this program and for the freedom that Step One has provided me, with God's help. It helped me begin a wonderful, lifelong journey toward recovery and serenity, with my Power Greater always at my side. As I keep growing, I gain new ideas and concepts that I wasn't ready for even a few months ago—at least that's how the process works for me.

## Step Two: Came to believe that a Power greater than ourselves could restore us to sanity.

The "came to believe" phrase in the Second Step has been a lifetime process for me. I've been reading and searching spiritually all of my life. Now I've come to believe that all I had to do all along was simply believe in God in a childlike manner. As an adult, I was a doubting Thomas. I spent a long number of years living in my head—chasing the answers, and trying to analyze the big *mystery of life;* asking God to give me directions and proof of His existence—just like Thomas. I feel now that His answer for me is "I really don't need to know." That insight from Him is a true blessing for me that continues to help me live serenely.

I was very insulted when my sponsor told me that in combating active alcoholism I had been using insane actions; going around in the same circles and directions, and expecting different results each turn I made. I felt at that time that there was nothing at all wrong with me; it was entirely the alcoholic's fault that our lives were miserable. I always thought I was the sane one in our relationship and knew what was right for our children and family in general. So I was very shocked to discover that I had been just as insane as my alcoholic, and even more so at times.

The miracle in this for me was that my brokenness made me vulnerable. That helped me become entirely willing to turn my life and will over to a Power Greater Than Myself, with complete trust that He could and would provide everything I needed, and even restore me to sanity. In my case, the insanity caused by living with the disease was the denial of my own needs and wants, as well as complete denial of the reality facing me on a daily basis.

As I look back on those years and think of all of the things I did or didn't do to try and make my children feel okay, I can see I was acting insanely a big part of the time. For example, I used a lot of "fits," conniving, ultimatums that I never followed through on. I spent every waking moment trying to figure out what to do about his mentality and behavior. I began to accept that my life was unmanageable; after all, I had tried everything possible to make it better, and nothing had worked. In fact, I began to realize that my insane behavior at times had only made some situations more unbearable for all of us.

I was forced to seek *new management.* The Twelve Steps in Al-Anon helped me to trust in my religious God. He had always been there for me, but I just never acknowledged that He was in charge of my life, and *had been all along.* I now ask Him every day to give me the courage, guidance, and vitality I need to get through the next twenty-four hours, and I am learning to "Let Go and Let God." That alone has been a big attitude adjustment for this Mary-Glen.

I was finally able to understand my part in all of the insanity of coping with the disease of alcoholism. My stinking thinking (Mary-my-way-be-done) had become my main coping tool. This Step promised me that, one way or another, I was going to get emotionally healthy. My biggest breakthrough came one day when I realized that part of the insanity I was unable to recognize while living with active alcoholism, was hoping to go back and make a happy childhood and have a mother who was very nurturing. What I do know today is that I no longer need to be anyone other than who I am. The only life I want is the one I have—just as it is.

The sanity part of Step Two meant gradually recognizing my inner voice and finally being able to trust it. For the longest time I doubted myself. There are still times when I do, but now I can sit back and know that the answers will come. If I can't find them, a Power Greater Than Myself will. Sanity now means being alive and embracing my life as it flows—with all of its ups and downs—and believing that no matter what happens, my God will give me the strength to handle it all. It is also the blessing of being completely honest about admitting my shortcomings, and the maturity and ability to recognize when I am using unacceptable behavior. With more years in the support groups, I've learned to change that behavior, and I now apply those principles to whatever God is sending my way "Just for today."

I've heard along the way that self-centeredness can prevent me from seeking a Higher Power. During most of my life, I felt that I didn't need anyone's help. I think that was the consequences of having too small an understanding of my God—and relying too much on my own perceptions of my capabilities. Today I can accept that I have human limitations.

## Step Three: Made a decision to turn our will and our lives over to the care of God *as we understood Him.*

I heard someone share an analogy recently about denial and the first three Steps. It's like being in a dark room with tightly shuttered windows preventing the sunlight from entering. (I intensely dislike rooms with heavy, closed drapes, and every room in our home is open to the view of outdoors.) I've also heard someone share in support groups that the world enlightenment breaks down to the *light of God* entering our Spirit. In Step Three I began to open up the shutters and let the light of my Power Greater enter. I love that analogy, because I love sunshine and I longed for peace and harmony around me, and I was willing to go to any lengths to get there.

I am very grateful that God led me to study different religions when I was younger, since it helped me understand the importance of spirituality in our program. I've belonged to an organized religion and church and had a strong faith in Him most of my life. *I believed* in God, but it never entered my mind to think about turning my whole life over to His complete care; inasmuch as I was too busy letting my will be done. I told Him, *"You mean I can actually do that, God? Wonder why I never thought about that before?"* I always had to feel that I was in control of everything so that it was sure to be done right—as I had planned, and as I thought it should be done! That was *self-will run riot*—just like the alcoholics. I was still trying to control the flow of life as God sent it each day.

Thinking of the flow of life reminds me of an awareness I received while we were at a fellowship convention in a hotel on the Colorado River in Laughlin. During a speaker meeting, we had chairs at the large picture windows that overlooked the river. While listening, I let my mind wander, watching the ducks as they tried to battle their way upstream against that quickly flowing river. They had to use all of their energy to make *any headway at all*; however, when they turned around and *went with the flow*, they were merrily on their way in the right direction. It became less of a struggle for them.

Sitting idly by, watching them that day, it reminded me of how much easier it is to go with God's will and plan for my life and surrender it all to Him. I find that keeps my focus in the moment-to-moment now, and that has become a daily delight for me. What a contrast to the days when I lived with my actively drinking alcoholic and I was habitually fearful, controlling, and despondent.

I had to change my attitudes from self-will run riot (defiance) to acceptance and surrender of all people, places, and situations that were unchangeable, but never the unacceptable (as in other's behavior toward me). That was the difference in the beginning. When I surrendered on bended knee to a Power Greater Than Myself, I was finally able to seek His Divine wisdom. Even while living in the confused and chaotic life I had after divorcing my ex-husband, and I was still trying to help him with his problems, I was able to find treasured quiet moments when I communicated with my inner Spirit.

I became willing to take action by trying to listen to God speak, in order to find my true inner being—the real self that He had created. To follow the will of a Power Greater Than Myself, I had to be willing to risk making mistakes. As a recovering perfectionist, that was difficult. Many times I had to "Let Go" *in the face of fear.* I'm more comfortable with the unknown now, and I can just let life surprise me as to what will happen next. Good listening means giving up my views, my perceptions, having trust and love in a Higher Power, and by following the example of others in the program. Only then did God give me the eyes to see what I needed—to see Him working in my life and that of others.

Freedom of self-will, meant that I was also able to be free of old negative behaviors and ways of thinking. (My mentor calls that emotional pollution.) I do need to retain some of my self-will, as my God allows me to have choices and do any footwork that's necessary for my welfare. The problem can (and does) arise when I allow my self-will to *conflict with His.*

When I began to pray only for a Higher Power's will, it meant that, finally, I started becoming the person He had intended all along. It's all been a part of a very active process for years now, of dedicating, committing myself to, and completely surrendering myself to something more wise and powerful than my humble being. When others share their solutions in meetings, it helps me immensely. But today I know that I have to pay attention to my own inner voice and discover what I feel is right and true for me.

A mentor told me an old tale which also convinced me it was time to take the risks to allow God to manage my will and life. It's the one about the drowning man who is going down for the third time, still refusing to take the hand of the man in the lifeboat for *fear that man will harm him.* The man in the lifeboat represents a Power Greater for me, and I had to trust Him and reach for His hand in order to step out in faith to face the world around me. Others in my Al-Anon Family taught me how to do that. A Twelve-Step old-timer told me that we don't have to climb all the way up to heaven to find a Higher Power. If we keep praying, He will find us—even "down in the basement!" I found that to be true in my life. He reached down and pulled me out of my mucky hole of misery and set me on a new path.

Others in my Twelve-Step groups convinced me that I truly have someone special in my Higher Power that I call God, who shows me unconditional love, and for the first time in my life I could experience that type of love because of having them in my life.

By finding acceptance in the first three Steps, I became aware that by not accepting what I could not change, I had been carrying around a lot of shame and blame in that marriage. It only set me up for denial, anger, bitterness, and hurt feelings. There were so much verbal abuse and physical violence I could have avoided, as well as unhappiness that I would not have suffered, if I had only stepped back and "Let Go and Let God." Obviously, I didn't know how to do that before finding Al-Anon.

As a child, I looked to God as "My Father in heaven." I adored my biological father; he was an angel, and I'm sure he still is. When I have to do Step Three on a daily basis, again and again, I like to think of God as my loving Father telling me, "Why don't you try doing it this way? It will work much better for you."

Which reminds me of a wee story I heard many years ago. The author is unknown to me, and I'm merely going by memory about the actual words. A father was watching his little boy trying to build a road for his toy truck out of dirt; however, there was a big boulder in the way. He kept pushing and shoving it, and his father watched his efforts, then quietly asked him, "Are you sure you are using all of your strength?" The little boy, exasperated, shouted, "Yes, I am." The father then gently said, *"No you're not; you haven't* asked me *yet."* I think of that story when I'm unwilling to *bother* my God by turning to Him for His help.

While working Step Three, I asked many old-timers, "How can I tell my will (Mary-my-way-be-done) from God's will?" I couldn't figure out how to discern the difference for my own benefit. The answer that made the most practical sense to me was from a dual member (a member of both programs) who said, "When you don't have to justify your actions to anyone, you are doing your Higher Power's will." This perspective has helped me to daily apply Step Three, and Step Eleven, in very concrete, practical terms in any challenges I face.

Before Al-Anon, my only way of communicating in prayer to God was to review all of the things of the present and ask Him to change it all for me—make all of the people in my life stop hurting me—make them loving, kind, and patient. *Just like me*, of course. It was always time for a pity party, but no one else was ever invited. I had to feel I was the only victim and martyr. I try to be careful when I pray now, "I only want Thy will to be done today," to be sure that I am not still asking Him to do what I think is best for me or for someone else I love; always, of course, with the best of intentions. Only He knows what someone needs.

Step Three applied to my relationships means now there are many times I have to pretend that I'm just a character in a play. My role is just to be peaceful and serene, not to worry about the parts the other actors play, and I should not condemn another actor's performance. I can only act out the part that He has assigned me. (This helps me also stay out of others stuff.) This is one of the best things I've internalized in the program from others, as it helps me in any situation; in personal relationships, in my service work, and with my family. It helps me also avoid being vacuumed into any other's emotions, and I remain more objective that way.

Others told me that I had to have belief before I could develop faith; therefore, I could simply *act as if* I believed in a Higher Power until I could really feel that presence in my life. It's been my experience in the program that little by little, we literally file information like this into our subconscious mind, then one day we wake up to the realization *that we are actually using it.*

The sanity part of the first three Steps is using complete honesty when admitting my shortcomings and the maturity and ability to recognize my own unacceptable behavior. I can then use what I've learned in the program to change it and try to apply those principles to whatever God is sending my way.

When I used to pray for God to change someone else, it blocked me from feeling His love and guidance. With the help of Step Three, when I prayed only for "knowledge of His will for me," He sent wonderful people into my life who loved me and showed me a better way to live. He comforted me when I was in emotional pain, and He gave me courage when I was so afraid of doing life on my own. He has allowed me all along to choose my own path—even if it is full of ruts and potholes. If I am seriously taking off in a wrong direction, He puts up a barricade of some sort and gets me back on the right track. Life has truly become awesome for me since I began to "Let Go and Let God" on a daily basis.

When I feel that I am in God's care, I can also feel safe about my future. It's in His Hands. Living in the present moment became a reality after the Third Step, turning my will and life over to the care of God, *as I understand Him.* Then I can believe that I am exactly where I am supposed to be every moment. When I gave everything I own and everything I am up to my God (it already belonged to Him anyway; I just hadn't acknowledged it), I was able to experience a sense of honest relief and inner peace that is still growing as I work the Twelve Steps. Once I was finally free of heavy burdens I'd been carrying around for what had seemed like forever, I could feel excited about being alive, and grateful for each day that God gave me.

With the help and Grace of a Power Greater Than Myself, I have developed a sense of dignity and self-worth and a new purpose in life. I am no longer compelled to feel the need to control—to be responsible—for everything and everyone else, nor do I expect someone else to take responsibility for me. I am finally free from "Mary-my-will-be-done."

With the help and support of others in my support group, and by working the Twelve Steps, God became a living reality for me. I can't touch or see Him, as we humans understand those words, but today I can hear His voice.

# 6

# *The Healing Steps: Four through Nine*

I have been affected by someone else's disease of alcoholism most of my life, and it has taken many years in the process of actualizing the Twelve Steps to begin healing. I think I've made peace with the past, then some issue will break open an emotional wound and I have to deal with it all over again. Thank God, I have close friends now in my support groups that help me in that process.

Most of my life, I continuously read all of the spiritual and personality self-help books I had time for. I kept trying to make myself acceptable to others in whatever way I could, but I continued to feel that I never measured up to the people I greatly admired. When I used self-talk, the busy committees in my head used to ridicule the affirmations I was posting on my mirror. They'd tell me, "You're beautiful? Who do you think you are kidding?" And so forth.

The healing steps (Four through Nine), and the help of other people in the program, helped me overcome that struggle. God can indeed do for me what I cannot do for myself, and He helped me believe that I'm a worthwhile, lovable human being. When memories of my past life flow into my today, I can decide which of them to delete and forget and which ones to cherish. I have made peace with my past, through working the healing steps with a program sponsor.

**Step Four: Made a searching and fearless moral inventory of ourselves.**

When my sponsor helped me work the Fourth, Fifth and Sixth Steps, she asked me to write about these questions:

- "Are there any shameful "skeletons" in my closet I should share about and deal with?

- Who Am I? What are my values? What are the behaviors I'd like to keep?

- What are the things I want to change?

- What is my purpose here?

To overcome my human failings (my shortcomings), I first had to know what they were. By eliminating any shortcomings, I can replace them with good qualities; with the result that I get to choose the person I want to become, with God's help and direction. The more I practice new thinking and behavior, the less my defects can control me.

I became very shy, sensitive, and introverted as a child, and the verbal and physical abuse made me withdraw inwardly with my feelings. I had wounds that were deeply rooted and had long lasting effects on my life before working the Steps. I think my experiences as a child gave me a more sensitive understanding of the pain I feel in others now—especially newcomers—as they share their feelings. A mentor of mine told me, "It is through our wounds that we find God." The healing steps allowed me to *let go* of shortcomings I'd held on to as survival skills so long that I've forgotten how to behave otherwise.

While working the healing steps, I decided, as part of my growth in recovery, I would pack up all of my old accumulation of extra knick-knacks from years gone by and other extra stuff I wanted to clean out of my cupboards, and make room to store things more efficiently. I have a new self now, and some old material things from the past were simply an emotional attachment. By holding on to them, I was clutching something that no longer existed. They were merely unhappy memories in my mind, and I had absolutely no further use for them. They no longer had reality, so I donated them to Safe Nest. They were simply taking up storage space in my home that could be used for living in the here and now, like all of my great program literature and audiotapes. I'm sure someone else is now finding pleasure from my cast-off souvenirs.

Doing that process helped me when working my healing steps. I decided I would also clean out the garbage of the past in my mind—the bitterness and resentments—and begin anew so that I could heal those wounds with forgiveness of all others and myself. When I cleared my mind of that extra clutter of things I'd rather forget, I was left with only pleasant memories to live with. An added benefit was that when I disposed of all the stinking thoughts in my mind, I was able to find valuable positive assets in my character to recognize, keep, and be proud of. Getting rid of clutter in any form is a true joy for me now.

As I understand it now, the "fearless moral inventory" mentioned in Step Four is a listing of our character traits and patterns of conduct from the point of view of wrong or right. After living with the disease of alcoholism for such a long time, I think my view of what was right or wrong was distorted in many ways. It took some time before I could be more objective about myself. Others taught me that I first had to detach myself from the alcoholic's problem; I couldn't take an honest inventory of myself until I stopped blaming others for *my* problems.

My sponsor told me that I had to write about the how or why aspects of certain things about my past experiences. For example: "In what way did that old issue have the power to affect my life today? And what was my part, if anything?" Putting all of this on paper helped me begin again, renewed in my faith in God and myself. I had to "whine and snivel" once and for all so I could be done with it all and move on with my new life.

I needed to learn to verbalize and communicate my thoughts and feelings to others, so my sponsor told me to write down what I was feeling. I used to write down how I felt and what I thought I could do about it, and then I'd call her and read it to her and we'd talk about it. At that time it was the only way I could verbally express and communicate my thoughts. (Ah…I have come a long way since those days.)

Later she had me write my recollections of my life (my story) from as far back as I could remember, which was when I was about three years old; then she asked me to make a resentment list as part of my Fourth Step.

I read my entire inventory to her and she had me destroy my notes when we finished, because that was the procedure her sponsor had utilized. As the years went by in the program, I regretted that we had eliminated those private, personal insights. I had spent almost a year on them and put a lot of thought and effort into it. But as I am thinking about that, I probably should be happy I did, because at that time that twenty-three-page inventory was more about "them"—all of the sadness and disappointments of the past that others had caused me to experience. In retrospect, I hadn't recovered enough to recognize *my part* in all of that misery, but I did the best I could at the time.

Since then, I have done other yearly Fourth Steps (daily at times!) and learned to leave all others out of my Fourth Step inventory process, so I could obtain a clearer reality of my own motives and attitudes in certain events. This helped me concentrate on finding solutions to problems, and not *contribute* to a problem. I had to love and accept myself completely before I could be fearless in doing a personal inventory. I had allowed others to trample over my soul until it became so buried in self-doubts that I had to dig deeply within to free it of all those restraints and begin loving myself. Part of being able to get there was the unconditional love others offered me in the meetings.

I am a recovering perfectionist; however, seeking perfection only led me to have lots of anxieties. They destroyed my every waking moment and had the power to keep me from having true joy in my life. I always threw away anything that had a flaw in it, and then I replaced it with something new. I've reached the conclusion doing that contributed to the reason I would literally beat up on myself most of my life—I have physical and emotional flaws. The healing steps gave me hope and nurturing, and that hope in my heart and soul led me to true healing and the belief that I am a worthwhile, though imperfect human being.

I spent the day at our State Assembly recently with other members in service. We had a great day of intensive brainstorming that left my mind very active that evening and I had a problem sleeping; I suffered lots of nightmares when I did manage to sleep. When I awoke, I realized that they were only dreams; I could forget them. I woke to the reality of a new bright day with my Higher Power and the precious people I love. What does that have to do with the healing steps? Well, that is what they accomplished for me. They helped me deal with the reality of past bad memories that had been recycling in my mind for many years; in the same way nightmares do.

In Step Four, with humility, honesty, openness and willingness, I was able to uncover not only my liabilities, but also my assets. When I made my shortcomings list in the Fourth Step, my sponsor asked me to name twenty good qualities—or talents (assets)—I owned. I could only come up with a few at that time, but she quickly rattled off the rest. Today, I see my assets/abilities/talents as gifts from a Divine Power that I can use not only in my service work, but to help newcomers and others in the fellowship.

I found through my own experience, and with others I sponsor, that the healing steps won't work to bring me what I'm yearning for—peace and harmony in my life—if there's something I will not do or give up for my own healing; especially if that "something" is my own self-will.

I have helped some of those I have sponsored look at the following issues while doing a Fourth Step: Is it possible that there might be a habit or indulgence (overeating, sexual addiction, gambling, compulsive spending, etc.) that I won't give up? Is there a person/s I refuse to forgive or I'll say to them "I forgive you, but." (We say in Al-Anon, everything after *but* is what keeps me from healing.) Those are the behaviors that can keep me from recovering if I allow them to, and can separate me temporarily from the God *of my understanding*. He never moves away, but sometimes I wander from Him.

When I was in my teens and early twenties I probably broke a few of the Ten Commandments in one way or another and I'm certainly not proud of that admission. In my Fifth and Sixth steps, I confessed all of those sins to my Higher Power, to myself, and to my sponsor. To admit the truth, I wasn't going to at first because I thought, "She'll never know the difference." Nevertheless, I did get the courage and told her these things, and she simply said, "We've all done things we're ashamed of, my dear, but God loved you while you were doing those things and He still loves you." That revelation from her, in itself, helped me forgive myself, and all others, and begin the process of healing, so I could have conscious contact with God and receive His will for my life.

**Step Five: Admitted to God, to ourselves, and another human being the exact nature of our wrongs.**
**Step Six: Were entirely ready to have God remove these defects of character.**

I was fortunate to have a sponsor who used a whole day's holiday from her work to go over the Fourth Step with me. At the end of that day she told me we had completed not only the Fourth Step, but also Steps Five and Six. That is also how I help those I sponsor now; however, I break the Fourth Step work into an hour or two each week for whatever length of time we need.

I found in Step Five that "admitted to myself" was the most difficult part. I'd been hiding behind a phony mask most of my life, pretending everything was just "fine" in my world behind closed doors at home. Not only did I have to reveal my genuine personality, I had to admit it to God and one other human being.

Gratitude is a major part of Step Six. By recognizing and cultivating my abilities (my talents), I am willing to let go of my defects. If I'm uncomfortable with my old behavior, then I'm more willing to change it. I have gone through some tremendous changes these past few years by using Steps Six and Seven.

My shortcomings had become my survival kit of tools that had made me feel safe in my battle—first with an abusive mother, then with the active disease of alcoholism. In my early years in the program, I couldn't see that I didn't need those tools any longer. I only knew they made me feel safe and that I had some sort of control of my own life. As a matter of fact, it's obvious to me now that I wasn't even aware that I had shortcomings!

## Step Seven: Humbly asked Him to remove our shortcomings.

I decided to do the Seventh Step, the first time around anyway, by taking my list (verbally) to my Church Community Reconciliation Services before Christmas that year. I thought that by doing that I could be sure God would hear me. (I thought I was so insignificant to Him in those days.) I discovered, when I finished that process, that I still didn't feel love and respect for myself. I felt like the words in a popular song when I was younger: *Is that all there is?*

Now, I feel that was the result of my old behavior of wanting to be perfect. Sad to say, I was still feeling that I was the only one to do all of the difficult work, and not ask for help. I had to be perfect, and the only way I could be perfect was to work, work, and keep beating up on myself trying to do just that. I have been a do-it-yourselfer all of my life, and I tried to learn everything I could from self-help books. Consequently, in Al-Anon at that time I kept going to many step-study meetings, listening, and trying to get insights and ideas on how to remove my shortcomings. *I intended to develop a plan for exactly how to do that.*

And then the light-bulb moment came when that soft, gentle voice from within told me, "Haven't you forgotten something, Mary? Step Seven states: Humbly asked *Him* to remove my shortcomings." Ah, another lesson in recovery from Mary-my-will-be-done was accomplished, another spiritual awakening my Higher Power had been patiently waiting for me to recognize.

I had tried to make a happy path for myself all of my life, but I did not succeed. As in the first three steps, in Step Seven I have a Power I can turn my life and will over to—including my shortcomings.

With the help of other members, I'm aware now that the Seventh Step truly is: "Let Go and Let God"; step back, simply trust, and stay in His waiting room. We all learn and grow at our own pace and accumulate little insights as we journey along the way.

We have a program saying: "Awareness is the first sign that we're on our way to recovery." Today I can look at life as it flows and see it all as part of my God's beautiful plan with many issues, wherein the lesson becomes more meaningful to me as time goes on. I believe I'll never be finished with work on the Steps, but it's productive work. I find I am able to concentrate more on what Mary-Glen is doing and less and less on what I perceive others *ought* to be doing.

I don't look at Steps Four through Seven now as a dirty laundry list of wrong doings of myself, or others. Rather, it's a personal discovery of the authentic Mary-Glen, so that from this day forward I become my genuine self only; not what someone else thinks I should be based on society textbook images.

I believe I'll always be working on my human failings, but as my favorite Scottish poet Robert Burns wrote, "Oh would some power the giftie (God) give us, to see ourselves as others see us." If God had been able to do that in the beginning of working my program, I don't think I could have handled it at that time. He is using His power, albeit slowly, to show me what I am truly like as a person and what I need to continually work on and change.

## Step Eight: Made a list of all those we had harmed, and became willing to make amends to them.

Making amends in Steps Eight and Nine is part of the healing process, and I attempt to make peace with mistakes I've made in the past. However, making amends is not meant to be self-punishing in any way; they are actions I take that will benefit some others and myself. I don't use these steps in an attempt to make peace with my past about something that will be to someone else's detriment (a promiscuous affair, etc.). In my work on Steps Eight and Nine, my sponsor and I decided that my biggest amends were to God and myself.

The amends to Him were made because I had lost trust in His ability to help me, due to having had many prayers I thought had gone unanswered, and to myself for having lost all self-love and respect.

With the help of my great Twelve-Step sponsor, we decided that the best amends I could make to God and myself were to spiritually respond to those in need of help because of living with another's active disease. Those amends are a great joy for me today.

## Step Nine: Made direct amends to such people, except when to do so would injure them or others.

In the Ninth Step, there is a phrase: "…except when to do so would injure them or others." I have to include myself in the others. My sponsor asked me if I could now recognize instances when my minding someone else's business may have harmed someone. That is exactly what I needed to hear, and it was what I had done. I minded his business (my active alcoholic husband) and did things for him that he needed to do for himself.

I also tried to behave in such a way that he would not get angry since I was afraid of his violent temper. Rather than look at my own fears, or even why I would continue to live with him, I tried to control the situations and *made his pain and unhappiness mine.* I also harmed myself by obsessing about him so much that I totally ignored my own needs and accepted behavior that was unacceptable.

These things are all part of the reasons to continuously make amends to myself now.

In the process of doing my Step Nine, I thought about making certain amends to my divorced husband, but to do so would have possibly put me in harms way—physically, mentally, spiritually, and emotionally. That is when and why I was taught by others to drop the "a" off amends and simply *mend* my ways. Whatever my behavior or attitude was at the time that caused me to think I needed to make those amends, I realized that a changed attitude can help in making them, not directly, but in the way I treat new people in my life when a similar situation arises. The old behavior is left behind and the program principles are exhibited to others in the manner in which I handle relationships. I am no longer my former self, and I look back in complete disbelief at some of the things I did many years ago, before working the Twelve Steps.

I have been on the receiving end of others' amends. I listen very quietly to what they have to say, and then just give them a big hug. I don't question, or argue, or say, "this is not necessary," for I know it is necessary to them to make them. Some amends are made for us to cleanse our guilt and our souls, and yet *not have to be acknowledged by that individual*—which is okay. I made them, then moved on with a changed attitude. Other amends were made, accepted, and again I moved on, spiritually closer to my Power Greater for my efforts.

There are people I have to be with at times that I wish would change, and that they'd make Ninth Step amends for some of their behavior, or do something to make it right. The truth is, it doesn't matter if they do that or not, for I am the one who holds the tool that will heal those situations. First of all, because I should not be judging them, and even if they did apologize, I would still have to be willing to forgive them. Back to one of the basis slogans of our program— "Keep the focus on me." I have to remember not to expect others to be responsible for my Serenity. I must release (*let go*) judging others' behavior and show them compassion, as I hope they do me. God forgives everyone and understands us. I should do the same, say my own prayer asking for forgiveness, and try to be a good example.

I see the healing steps today as tools that are used by a Higher Power to repair damage to my soul. I first had to hate the thoughts or actions that were blocking me from receiving His wisdom, before I could overcome the damage done. When I was able to give up whatever I was getting out of my old survival skills, my shortcomings, only then was I able to admit my dependence on a Power that is great and good beyond anything I can imagine or understand.

By using true humility, I feel a big load has been taken from me when I am able to amend my wrongs today. I avoid a lot of disagreements with others now when I have the courage to simply say: "I made a mistake," "I apologize," or "I was wrong."

I am sure I still have many painful lessons to walk through and learn from, but I am slowly recovering, with the help of the fellowship. I just keep putting one foot in front of the other (known in the program as the footwork), and follow My Power Greater Than Myself. Healing a broken Spirit didn't—and won't—happen overnight. It has taken me lots of time and effort and dedication to my program.

With the help of the healing steps—Step 4 through Step 9—I stopped having anxieties about trivialities, and I try to use each day as if it were my last to live on this earth. I look for all of the love and laughter I can find, and my beloved husband now reminds me constantly, "This is the first day of the rest of our lives. Things will turn out the way they're supposed to, but only when they are supposed to."

# PART III

## The Use of the Program Principles

# 7

*A Feeling of Belonging*

*When knowledge becomes understanding, I am more able to use the principles of the steps as actions. Mary-Glen Scot.*

I am not in Al-Anon because someone's drinking was a problem for me, nor because I'm now married to a twenty-four-year-sober alcoholic. Rather, I'm a member because I needed a reason to continue living—hope for a new way of life.

I always wanted to be part of a big, loving family, and I am now. I lived in isolation most of my life, and in Al-Anon I found the family that I always longed for as a child—warm, loving, gentle, and nurturing. My soul made me feel there was something I was missing in life, and I had spent most of my life searching to see if I could fill that void with creative hobbies, church, or by reading spiritual books.

I remember pleading with my parents to buy me a second-hand leather-bound copy of *Pilgrims Progress* when I was fourteen. (That was my one and only birthday present; they were both misers.) I found a new copy at a bookstore recently, and I scanned through it. It is a very old spiritual book and difficult to read; for the life of me, today, I can't determine today why I wanted that book. Maybe I had heard someone talking about it, or perhaps it was all part of God's plan for me.

When I was led to the program, I found what I'd been searching for to fill that inner emptiness and yearning. The people in the program helped me accomplish what I couldn't do in a lifetime of searching by myself. If you have just joined a Twelve-Step program, please don't leave until you experience your first miracle.

My Higher Power didn't stop at one miracle, and I'm sure yours won't either. My first miraculous awareness was being filled with a sense of belonging.

We have a very diverse membership in my program. My first meeting was in a church with about ten people present, and most of them had been meeting at that location for about ten years. I learned much later that one lady was a lawyer, one man a professor at UNLV, and one had her own successful business. That's one of the things I love most about the program: It doesn't matter what our professions happen to be; when we walk through the door into a meeting, we are anonymous, and that makes us all equal, but unique human beings.

The next meeting was entirely different. It was in an older part of town in an A.A. club, which means some A.A. members had purchased the premises privately and rented the rooms to Alcoholics Anonymous members, and some Al-Anons/Alateens for their meeting places.

I drove up, saw rows of *Harley Davidsons* and big, rough-looking bikers (members of A.A.), all standing there in front of the door I had to enter. Most of them were talking loudly and smoking, and I thought, "Oh dear Lord, do I have to walk through that crowd?" I almost drove around them and left again, but I stayed and I went there to a meeting every day for six years or more. Those tough bikers became my angels in many ways. (No pun intended there.) They used to lovingly direct me if I had a problem getting around all of their parked bikes, and bodies when I left my meeting.

In that particular support group, we had only one meeting all week there because the rest were Alcoholics Anonymous. The old sofas sagged down to the floor when we sat in them, and were pretty grungy, to say the least. We had a few drunks wander in and fall asleep on the old sofas, and one used to pass out and snore very loudly while we were sharing! Ah, those were the days; however, I learned more about life and the Twelve-Step program in a year or two in those particular two meetings I've just described than I ever could have anywhere else.

We had a membership of about forty people in each of those meetings, a lot of them dual members (both A.A. and Al-Anon), and we'd go out for coffee afterwards. Every one of them made me feel that I belonged. We called it "the meeting after the meeting." Prior to that time, I always felt that I did not fit in with anyone, anywhere, and now I had this big, loving, caring family that I had always longed for while growing up. The miracles of this great program were just beginning for me, and I wasn't yet aware that God had many more in store for me.

I prayed a lot to my Higher Power when I separated from my husband. The following prayer is a very simple one I used in the beginning, and if you are going through a grief process of any kind, it may help you also: "Father, I'm going through a big loss right now and feeling very alone and helpless. I need you to show me you are really there, but above all, Thy will be done." This prayer helped me clarify what was bothering me and to know that He *would* share the burden with me. I no longer felt alone or helpless. Prayer is a Power Greater's gift to all of us, and when I learned how to use it, my problems became easier to handle.

I came to my first meeting numb, fearful, timid, very confused about where I was heading, and completely lost. I felt I had no control over my life. I desperately needed to find a better way to live, and the loving people in the fellowship gave me all of the love and support I needed. I simply listened to everyone and cried in the beginning. I really didn't know what or how to share. I'd kept my feelings locked up for so long, I didn't know how to begin.

One of my major risks in recovery was taking down my big protective wall I'd built around me that had a big sign printed in red: "Don't come too close; you might hurt me." I was so afraid of allowing others into my heart—afraid they would reject me and/or betray me. I had extremely low self-esteem, but I hid it quite well, and no one knew how fragile I was under my fake, well-practiced smile. How could they? I was so busy care-giving everyone else's feelings, needs, and desires that I ignored mine entirely.

My wall had kept others at a distance, but it forced me to stay isolated. I lived behind that false façade most of my married life to the actively drinking alcoholic, and I had never had close women friends. Little by little, the disease had been taking its toll on me, ripping me apart and tearing me down with it. It was winning the battle, and that made it difficult for me to keep that false smile.

When I lived in denial, I became like an ostrich; I pretended our problems would go away if I just covered them up. I lived the illusion that I could avoid the world and its challenges. I never thought to look within myself to find relief from *our* problems. My life became one of keeping the focus on him—the actively drinking alcoholic. As a result, over a period of many years, my anxieties, fears, and husband became a personal power greater than I was. Eventually, others in the program educated me not to accept inappropriate behavior, and deal with the problem of active alcoholism instead of playing sick games.

In that first marriage, there was seldom any loving, meaningful communication with my husband—by his choice. It's sad for me to think about that now. His parents were both dead by the time he was twelve years old, and accompanied by an older sister, he came to live with an aunt in Los Angeles. An older brother later joined them. One evening, his brother shared some of their childhood memories with me about how their father would get drunk and throw their mother on the floor and kick her. I questioned my husband later about that because he seldom spoke about his life before marrying me, and all he would say was, "Yes, he was a bastard." I spent most of my life living with him, and yet I never really knew or understood him emotionally—what he was ever truly feeling about himself, life, or me. *Perhaps he never even knew that himself.*

Unfortunately, his mind and thinking processes are now very deteriorated because of the years of heavy alcohol consumption, and he lives in a rest home. No one may ever be able to determine what his true inner self is like. Alcohol is cunning, baffling, and it destroys everything it comes in contact with. It did destroy our relationship; it took many years, *but it won.*

There finally came a time when I could not just *act as if* I were fine any longer, but the program worked miracles for me. After a lot of difficult work and reflection about keeping the focus on me, my Higher Power revealed to me (and I came to believe) that I am a worthwhile person. I ever so slowly began taking my wall down. Brick by brick, those barriers were removed, and I began to trust the people in the program. By doing that, I was able to feel fairly safe as I allowed others to get to know parts of the genuine me. At some point, I became willing and ready to feel strong and secure enough to share my whole true inner being with some members I felt I could trust. Later, I was able to reach out to everyone I possibly could in my Twelve-Step Support Family. Problems are opportunities for growth, and I instinctively reach out to others now, instead of isolating.

Most of my life, I had never practiced the habit of looking into people's eyes as I spoke with them. I used to look to the right or left of them. Obviously, I had never learned to communicate in a meaningful way. I remember one of my first shares in a meeting; I kept looking down, nervously stumbling for words, in tears, and apprehensive as to whether or not I was sharing correctly. When suddenly, my eyes connected with someone else. There it was—the eyes said, "It's all right" and the intent gaze said, "I am listening." The soft smile on her face told me, "You are safe; I understand." This person was listening with true love and compassion, and it came across the table to comfort me, without her saying a word. Then I noticed the nodding heads of others, as if they too were saying, "Continue, you're doing okay." Later they gave me their hugs, and that one special lady took my hand and said very simply, "I understand." She will never know how much that meant to me. (The same lady became my sponsor six months later.)

I believe that was the beginning of my understanding and feeling of true intimacy in communicating with others. Today, I make sure that I look into someone's eyes when I communicate with them one-to-one. Besides which, I've learned with the help of this great program, that when I look in their eyes I see my God, and I hope they will see theirs in mine.

I was encouraged by loving people in this program to be gentle with myself. I also found out that it was okay to make mistakes. That's allowed; I'm only human. As a result of working this program and being surrounded by people who encouraged me and understood me, I slowly began to heal from old wounds and doubts. I started to feel better about and actually like myself. Little by little, I began to see the gifts that a Higher Power had given to me. I began to see myself in a healthier way—good and bad qualities—and my confidence started to grow.

Because of the pain I have gone through in my lifetime, my Power Greater has given me the gift of a loving and compassionate Spirit. I can easily understand and feel another's sadness or joy. I love people, and I really enjoy listening as they share their feelings with me. The great factor is that this program has taught me how to take these gifts (and others) I have received from God and make them grow. I have learned how to extend my compassion to all people, including the alcoholics in my life. I can still love them, but hate their disease. If I keep daily conscious contact with my Him, everything else just falls into place.

My Twelve-Step family helps me feel accepted for who I am, and not what society thinks I *should be/could be*. It means I am part of a family of unconditionally loving people who have a never-ending circle of love, with our Higher Power in the center. He sends his love to us; we give it to each other, and send it back to Him again. I am no longer sitting outside looking in, feeling very alone in the world, wondering what my purpose is in life and where I fit in.

There is an old spiritual saying: "What you are is God's gift to you; what you make of yourself is your gift to God." These words inspire my heart and soul today and I try to apply them in working my program. The program has taught me to feel my feelings, embrace those feelings, embrace reality, and that I can become the person I was destined to be. Al-Anons talk about *working the program*, but I think that, after a while, *the program simply started working me*.

In the beginning, it was painful at times, discovering the real me, myself, and I, after being asleep in denial about my own needs for such a long time. I still felt a great longing and need to be loved and accepted. Maybe you wouldn't even like me if I showed you my true inner being in an honest, open manner. About that time, a program member told me, "You will only learn to understand as much of yourself as you are willing to share with others." My experience in the fellowship has convinced me there is truth in that statement.

I think the memories of bad past experiences before beginning the program kept committees going in my head that told me, "Don't trust anyone." I had never before dared to be open about who or what I was, but in the beginning, the fear of rejection made me hesitant to share what I thought and felt—what I was *really* thinking and feeling, not what I thought others *wanted or expected* me to share. I had lived in isolation for a very long time, and in Al-Anon I learned to break that silence and speak to others about what was on my mind.

When I reveal myself honestly and openly, I am revealing who I am, where I am, and what I am all about. That was scary; I'm a recovering perfectionist! Today, I know I don't have to measure up to your standards or the image of perfection of myself that I used to strive for. By sharing of my true self I was able to break through all those years of isolation and living in a fantasy world, to finally be able to face the realities of what God is sending my way.

My greatest challenge wasn't learning to love others; it was learning to let them *love me*. When I made myself be honest and intimate with others in my sharing in the meetings, I never felt alone again. Verbalizing and sharing the dark secrets in my soul let me begin to heal.

Gradually, I began to change, but before I could move forward I had to release myself from the bondage of thoughts of what I thought I'd done wrong in the past. I can recall many simple little things I'd said or done wrong (in my eyes) in my life that embarrassed me. The sad thing is, I'm positive that no one else probably even noticed at the time it happened. (The reality is that emotionally healthy people would have realized it had nothing to do with them.) But those things kept coming back to haunt me, and I always seemed to be at war with myself.

I'm also a romantic idealist and I always thought everyone in the world should live in peace and harmony! Well, I had to wake up, face reality, and tell myself, "Life is just not that way, Mary." Other members taught me that I could be loving and kind to myself, and that was the only way I could find the real me behind that outward façade I had created.

I had to finally forgive myself and get rid of those old audio and videotapes stored in my mind and stop reviewing them. I was in a big mucky hole of sadness when I came to the Twelve-Step program, and it took time and all of their love and support to start climbing out of it. I had judged, convicted, and sentenced myself to go there. I can't blame anyone but myself; I was my own worst enemy. I continually chaired a committee in my head that loved to be critical of me.

I grew up somehow with the idea that I was expected to be responsible for and take the blame for everything, good or bad, which happened around me. I'm sure that could all be attributed to my insanity from living with the disease. I had to struggle to change my stinking thinking of a lifetime, and Step Two helped me do that. When I began the process of forgiving myself in the healing steps—I was able to fire all of those self-critics. It took the miracle of love from others in the fellowship to convince me that what I did in the past has little to do with the person that I now am. I began by forgiving the person I was, accepting who I am today, and loving the person I am becoming.

Alcoholism is cunning and baffling, and living with it had affected me so drastically that I had almost lost the desire to live. The people in the program helped me to cherish, honor, love, and respect myself, and then I could treat all others in that same manner. By truly appreciating my uniqueness and talents, I learned to believe that I could value and become the person I wanted to be. Even with my mistakes, I'll go to any lengths now to keep the self-respect and dignity that I've gained with the help of the fellowship.

My life is happier today because I learned to listen and trust the experiences of others in the program. I don't have to find out everything for myself the difficult way and try to do life on my own. If I keep my main focus on my Power Greater Than Myself, I am given unlimited opportunities for personal growth. With a lot of enthusiasm for God and this wonderful program, I can give out positive energy that can be received by others. Not only do I create an atmosphere around me of love and harmony, but I feel also that it has a definite influence on others today.

When I have H.O.W. (Honesty, Openness and Willingness), there's always something new each day for me to discover and enjoy. An old saying is *want* power makes *will* power. We say in our program, "If you want what we have and are willing to go to any lengths to get it, you will find help and make progress." We have to find the willingness before we can first begin. The people in the support group gave me unconditional love, taught me how to laugh, how to rebuild my life, and have a high level of self-confidence I've never experienced.

If you happen to be fairly new to a Twelve-Step program, please don't ask yourself: "How do I compare with someone else in the program?" Rather, ask: "How far have I come from where I began?" That is what is most important. I'm positive that I've reached the other side of my mountain now (most of the time anyway). It's my humble opinion that it's not the number of years in the program that shows our growth; it's how much effort one is willing to put into working the principles in all relationships—intimate or otherwise. We don't only intellectualize the Steps with a sponsor; we actualize them (live them), and that will reflect in our recovery.

It is only through close friendships with other women in Al-Anon that I am now able to say, "This is who I am" and "This is what I am feeling." I think my spirituality began with knowing my own truths and not that of anyone else, and I have to share those truths in our meetings.

I love analogies, and this one came to me in my beginning work on the Twelve Steps: When I studied the Scriptures, I recall how some of the tribes of Israel had wandered in the desert for forty years and were finally led to a paradise. This led me to think of my own forty years fighting the battle of alcoholism. I think of my recovery journey along the way as if I had been going across a barren desert, and I could see this beautiful oasis in the distance, but I wasn't quite there yet. That "oasis," when I arrived there, was my Serenity—the peace, love, and harmony in living—that big mystery of life I had been searching and yearning for all of my life.

# 8

# *Acceptance and Using the Serenity Prayer*

*"God, grant me the serenity*
*To accept the things I cannot change,*
*Courage to change the things I can,*
*And Wisdom to know the difference."*

**"I will pray more, work the program more, and leave the rest to**
**God." (Author anonymous.)**

Prayer is not asking for my wishes to be granted; it's praying for His will to be done. It's okay to want what I want, as long as I put God's will above my own desires.

We begin all of our meetings in Al-Anon with a moment of silence (while we pray for those who haven't found us yet), and then we recite the Serenity Prayer. Part of it that we don't use in our meetings (and sometimes I wish we did as a reminder) states: "Trusting that He will make all things right if I surrender to His will." Trusting and believing in a Power Greater Than Myself has been my greatest gift of the Twelve-Step program, and I have to stay grounded, plugged into, and connected to that Power that I'm positive will never fail me. Al-Anon is my lifeline to that Power.

I am grateful for the gift of the Twelve-Step program because of the tools it gives me, one of which is the Serenity Prayer. During the time I was dealing with active alcoholism in my former husband, I spent most of my days feeling fear, anger, resentment, self-pity, and in complete contempt of him. I used to pray to God to stop him from drinking, and I kept all of my focus on the alcoholic's problems. I was filled with melancholy, loneliness, and a yearning for something—I didn't know what.

My soul kept longing for a better way of life. I tried to fill those longings with compulsive shopping (also known as retail therapy), obsessing about other people, and by trying to fix their faults. (Take their inventory.) I finally learned to concentrate on my own behavior, and it wasn't 'til I started working to know what my needs and wants were that I began to heal.

The wisdom I'm looking for, to "know the difference" in the Serenity Prayer comes from prayer and meditation, meetings (one or more daily if possible), sponsorship, reading program literature, listening intently to others sharing in meetings, writing my thoughts daily, and all of this has been extremely healing. I am able to open my heart with more love and compassion for others than I did before working the Twelve Steps, for a Higher Power gave me the courage to change the things I can—my own attitude and behavior—and that does take a lot of perseverance. When I pray for acceptance and courage, eventually the wisdom will come, and I truly will know the difference between what I can change and what is entirely in God's hands.

I really feel like I am making progress, and the program gives me *guidelines*; not a timetable for change. It's comforting and reassuring to know I am able to accept and change myself at my own pace. I realize now, many years later, that the majority of things I was dealing with on a daily basis had little to do with the affects of coping with alcoholism; rather, they had to do with my inability to accept the reality of what life was sending my way. I had to find the desire to want healthier ways of living, and actually do something about it for myself. The use of the Serenity Prayer helps me accomplish this.

I sat through my first meeting, listened to others who offered their ESH (Experience, Strength, and Hope), and felt the warmth of their hugs as I drove home that evening. I still remember the feeling of being offered unconditional love, and it stayed with me until I got home. It was a feeling I had not had for so very long, except from our precious daughters.

I'll have to be honest here and tell you that the feelings didn't last long; because I had a very angry active alcoholic waiting for me at the place I still had to call "home." However, I had a glimpse of what this program could give me if I kept coming back. Thereafter, that same feeling of inner peace lingered with me as I left each meeting, and each time it seemed to last a little longer. Finally, I learned how to get that feeling back if I lost it. I did that with the use of the telephone to call other members for suggestions, and reading program literature when life got hectic. Six months later, I had my first sponsor and began working the Steps.

Other Al-Anons taught me how to satisfy my own needs, how to create a life that brought me happiness as well as peace, and not feel guilty about it. If I do feel any guilt, I am able to turn it over to the God *of my understanding*, reason it out with a program friend or my sponsor, and then let it go. I'm a work in progress and can still fall into old thinking and behavior; however, as soon as I feel my serenity and peace slipping away from me, I do whatever it takes to bring back that calmness in my soul.

A program mentor told me to make sure I took time for solitude. In what other way could I meditate and be grateful for the blessings in my recovery? In the beginning, others told me to surrender my self-will to a Power Greater Than Myself and become willing to accept whatever he/she puts in front of me. I only began to experience the peace that surrender can bring by practicing it in my daily contact with all others. Everything in life I have had to learn through doing it over and over again, so that makes a lot of sense to me, and I'm sure it will to you also. I had to continuously practice my piano to get to a higher level (no pun intended); and I also have to practice my program of Twelve Steps on a continuous basis if I hope to reap all of the benefits from it.

I find that many times I can escape an unhappy situation—temporarily at least—by going to my inner sacred sanctuary, a secret garden I've created in my mind's eye. I loved the children's story by that name about the little girl who found an old, neglected, hidden garden. It had a large brick wall surrounding it, and she found a carefully hidden, rusty key to the old wooden gate leading into it. In the remake of the movie a few years ago, the garden looked just as I had always pictured it, because it is absolutely heavenly—full of sunshine, fragrant flowers, and the song of the birds. I use that beautiful image now when I need to find tranquility. I say the Serenity Prayer and mentally go there until I can find my composure to deal with whatever challenge is facing me.

Sometimes I have to practice acceptance and surrender with health problems, and I can say I truly feel serene when I do. I know that I cannot have true joy in my life unless I have gone through some emotional or physical pain somewhere along the way, and I can use whatever I'm learning to share with others.

I've received so much out of this program; simply by listening and accepting the insights others offer in their sharing in meetings. There are many times when I hear things that I can't relate to—even want to argue with them, but often, in

God's time, those same things make total sense and end up helping me. I often take what I like and leave the rest, and then some of that rest comes to me later when I need it. I believe that my Higher Power used the people in Al-Anon to carry me when I felt at times that I couldn't walk through the emotional pain any longer. It took one day following another, sometimes one moment at a time and one small step at a time, to get where I am today.

Serenity is not a final destination, nor a retreat, in the sense that I don't arrive there and never face tribulations again. I believe it means adjusting my attitudes and behavior to daily life as it occurs. The Serenity Prayer helps me with acceptance of life and the spiritual journey I travel, and that is probably my main focus in maintaining serenity during crisis situations.

I also have a new meaning for a "crisis." It used to be anything that didn't go my way, or life just happening as it does. They were all huge crises! Now I can distinguish between what is truly a crisis versus what is merely an inconvenience to me; therefore, there aren't as many crises to weather. Thanks to my program family and God, I can find peace even amidst the chaos. A member gave me a floral laminated bookmark with "How important is it?" when I first began working the Steps, and it has been hanging on our refrigerator ever since as a reminder. Paul jokes that it is there to remind him whenever he goes to the freezer for the ice cream!

I've heard many times in meetings that, wisdom is not knowledge; wisdom is the ability to separate truths from false facts. The difference is whether to act to change something, or relax and accept things as they are—then give it to God. Through good and bad times these words have proven to be an invaluable inspiration in my recovery. Today, "the wisdom to know the difference" in the Serenity Prayer brings new meaning and purpose as I seek to live on life's terms, and for that I am grateful. Also, in my senior years, I believe that wisdom is knowing that I cannot slow the passing of time, nor can I make certain events occur before His Divinely appointed time. I'm happy to realize this because *what ifs* and *if only* thoughts are guaranteed to send me "NUTS." (Not Using the Steps. I love acronyms.)

The Twelve Steps have helped me accept my past and not keep wishing I could go back and change it all. I've also learned that there are many places, people, and situations I have absolutely no control over. I have choices, but I don't have to try to control other's choices; especially my close loved ones. God has a master plan for my life, and the people and circumstances He sends into my life are all part of His plan. I must keep working on the need to accept life as it is, and then I will have contentment one moment at a time. I believe it's a matter of constantly telling myself the saying from our program: "Don't fear tomorrow, for

God is already there." I have a firm faith in living in the present and in those words, and I do have peace and contentment with my life as it flows today.

I pray for acceptance and courage every time I use the Serenity Prayer. Eventually, the wisdom does come from my inner voice or something someone shares in a meeting. But however it comes, I'll know what's mine to handle and what belongs in God's hands. I am beginning to be more and more aware of my own inner voice telling me: "This is my will—not God's." With the wisdom I've gained from working the Steps, I am learning the difference between the two. This makes my life so much easier today. I can pray now that my former husband will find his own Higher Power inside his own soul. I can do no more than that for him, and I have peace with that decision today.

I've weathered many storms; however, as they do in nature, storms gradually end, and so do severe challenges in my life. With the help of my personal Power Greater, I can accept what is happening in the moment by remembering that whatever I'm experiencing will soon reach its end. The problem itself is worsened by my fear and panic during a crisis, if I allow it to overwhelm me. Like the changing of the seasons, crisis does end in just one simple moment at a time. I can accept what is happening, understanding that the crisis I find myself in at this moment in time *will* come to an end, and I will have grown; no matter what the outcome. It is the fear of the outcome in a crisis that throws me into panic, yet I have heard it said so many times, "Let go of the outcome and concentrate on the journey, for the journey carries the lesson and the outcome will be what it will be." I still find this difficult, but I am working on it one day at a time.

It's easier to have acceptance in a crisis when I am in a position to be reminded by a sponsor or other member of the program of a great program phrase: "Absolutely nothing happens in my Higher Power's world by mistake," and our slogan: "This too shall pass." There are many lessons in all of my difficulties (caused by my own self-will at times) that bring me strength, and understanding to get me through whatever God is flowing my way. The Serenity Prayer leads me to ask for God's help, be quiet, listen, and wait. *The answers will come.*

The most important thing I learned from my old actions and behavior is that my prayers to God need not be for emergencies only. Before working the Steps, I had an imaginary emergency 911 alarm, and I'd push the panic button when I had a big crisis, then shriek, "Oh God, please help." Practicing self-reliance, independence, and sheer determination left me in a mucky hole of misery. Now I know that I can ask God for help at anytime and He will respond, sometimes immediately, if I am in real distress. *I've discovered the miracle and wonder of prayer.*

By letting my Higher Power be in charge and keeping an open, willing, mind, He helped me accomplish things that I never dreamed I could. I even took my first flight on a plane after I began working the Steps. I had a horrible phobia about getting on an airplane, and I had avoided flying all of my life. I even thought when I was young that if I ever went back to Scotland I would go by train and by ship from New York. Only about a week or so to get there! When I first came to the fellowship, a member told me, "You can be scared to death and fly, Mary; you don't have to feel comfortable. Just buy the damn plane ticket! God will be the pilot, and He will be in charge" So I did. The first time I flew, I thought it was one of my greatest spiritual experiences ever. I had never felt so close to a Higher Power, which I think tends to prove the program saying, "Belief is the fuel that allows you to fly." (And I did!)

I've learned that I have a right to make choices based on what's right for me, and what others think of my choices is none of my business. What freedom that offers me. What peace I'm given when I live my life that way; a life that is honoring to my inner being and God. Life can still get unmanageable, but the tools of this program are with me throughout my day.

Now when I pray for acceptance, I know I cannot change anyone, and the issue whatever it may be is safely in God's hands. That definitely takes a big load off my shoulders. By accepting the burdens of the things I cannot change, He gives me the strength to handle any difficulties I encounter along my path to serenity. The program has taught me that acceptance goes beyond tolerance. Acceptance respects the worth and dignity of each and every human being, as God does me.

Acceptance has grown to be a solution to many problems for me; however, in some situations, making changes is possible and even desirable for those involved. In those, acceptance means I have to take responsibility, the action, and have willingness on my part to do whatever footwork may be necessary.

Just because I accept my own powerlessness to change a person, place, or circumstance doesn't mean I can't have hope for my own future, or that I don't have choices in any troubles I face. Today, my action—emotionally and/or mentally—in a vulnerable situation is to place it all in a greater Power's hands. I can ask for His guidance in deciding what needs to be done, determine what my part entails in getting that accomplished, and ask for His strength to help me carry that out. Nevertheless, I'm convinced today that God never expects me to be submissive in any degrading situation with which I am faced.

My main ideal definition of serenity today would be, *the peace that surpasses all human understanding*, and I believe that means it would be indescribable in words. I believe now that serenity, as elusive as it can sometimes be, is a feeling deep down inside of me where I am at peace with God, my fellow man, and myself.

Faith and trust in a Higher Power has greatly grown with help from my program. I discovered that when I keep an open mind, I see His Spirit working through others and myself, and that is the beauty of any Twelve-Step program.

I'm still not positive whether or not serenity is a state of mind, as such. I can't intellectualize my way into a serene state of mind. I think it's the result of a state of being—being in the present, being content with my life just as it is, and as I am, and not wishing for a different past or longing for things to be different today. I can still have dreams and goals, but my future is in God's hands and big plan for me.

# 9

## *Alcoholism—The Disease*

Acting with contempt, disgust, criticism, leads to broken relationships, so we must try to have compassion for the person who is caught up in the disease. I had to convert my former pain from living with the disease into wisdom, growth, hope and trust in a Power Greater Than Myself.

When I lived with an actively drinking alcoholic, he could always find some sort of excuse why he had to drink more and more. In the program, that's known as the "blame game." There will always be something that gets blamed, whether it be a spouse, parents, children, maybe work, traffic, something or someone made it worse that day, or that week, or that month, and the alcoholic has an excuse to drink, again.

As a newcomer, I didn't like our Twelve-Step phrase: "Keep the focus on yourself and not on the alcoholic." I wanted to know how I could encourage and support the alcoholic in my life so that he would be the way I wanted him to be, for only *then* could I be happy! My life became unmanageable with that type of distorted thinking, but thank goodness, I just kept coming back to the meetings. When we practice one principle of the program for a month or more, we are more likely to own it.

In the beginning of working the Twelve Steps, I found it easier to be compassionate in dealing with someone's alcoholism if I were in a good spiritually, emotionally, physically healthy place myself. (The acronym and slogan "HALT" applies here. "Don't let yourself get too Hungry, Angry, Lonely, or Tired.") However, it was difficult to have compassion for others when I was in a state of self-pity or whatever, because that was when I needed to be giving it to myself first. Ah…back to square one: "Let it begin with me."

Program-wise, I had little to offer others, but I didn't know that in my early days of recovery. I thought I had lots of answers for others and so much to share because I had put so much effort into studying program literature. I didn't realize at that time that I could grow more readily by putting into use on a daily basis all of the principles of the program that I had been intellectualizing. We learn more by practice and doing than by simply memorizing something and repeating it at meetings.

Living with active alcoholism affected my mind and Spirit and created bad attitudes in me. By the Grace of God, my body doesn't have the constant demanding desire to be consumed by alcohol, but I had a closed mind about the disease itself, and I had no sympathy or understanding towards any alcoholics. (My soul is crying now, as I'm admitting that to you.) It was suggested that I attend open A.A. meetings, and I learned to really listen to the wisdom A.A. speakers shared about their lives (known as their "stories").

I have a different perspective about alcoholism now. If someone's drinking affects me, it's not up to me to label that person an "alcoholic." As with any disease, it is up to the person with the disease to make a decision about how to treat it, usually with the help of a professional person. Maybe we can present options; however, our Twelve-Step program helps us practice letting go so we may give the person freedom and the dignity to find help. It also helps us accept that *their Higher Power is guiding them where they need to go.*

A lot of my feelings in the past were somewhat similar to what the alcoholic goes through and thinks. They escape painful circumstances in their lives by using alcohol. I escaped the pain of living with active alcoholism by the denial of reality, and fantasizing just how our lives could be or would be some day. That day never came for me. Other members later taught me that *should be, could be,* or *would be* are definitely self-defeating thoughts.

I attend a weekly open A.A. speaker meeting of two to three hundred people with my husband. The speakers are flown in from around the U.S.A., and each one of them shares his/her own story of learning to control the disease. I learn a lot about alcoholism by listening to them, and I know that today I also have been emotionally affected by living with the active disease. The A.A people state that they have a "three-fold disease of mind, spirit, and body," and I also have a *three-fold problem,* mainly about bad attitudes, denigrating tone of voice, and distorted thinking. Some Al-Anons like to say they also have a "disease." I don't, for the reason I think that makes light of the alcoholics' problem. (Unless, of course, they happen to be a dual member.) A disease is described in a journal about alcoholism as an "involuntary disability." I feel I do not have a "disease," because I was absolutely a volunteer to it all!

I've since learned that if someone, or myself, has a loved one who has gone "back out" one more time to drinking (an A.A. expression), then this is the time to remember that it is the alcoholism, and not the alcoholic that is being manifested. I can dislike alcoholism intensely as the disease it is, but still have compassion for the person that is suffering. He/she is stricken with a compulsion so overpowering that it's way beyond his/her control. All I can do is offer up a prayer for them to a Power Greater Than Myself, and offer them love.

My experience has been that I couldn't have compassion for an alcoholic, or anyone else for that matter, until I had stopped judging myself so harshly. By changing my negative thoughts about myself, I was able to change my thoughts about others. Accept them just as they are by using our slogans, "Live and let live" and "How important is it?" as reminders. Only my Higher Power knows if someone/something is good or bad or not. The people in A.A. convinced me that no one in their right mind would willingly subject themselves to the consequences of prolonged excessive alcohol consumption. That information alone helped convince me that alcoholism is a disease and that I ought to be thankful that except for God's Grace—there go I.

In other instances, when I had trouble feeling compassion in any manner for another human being it was usually due to my being judgmental or arrogant. For example, thoughts of, "If they would just behave as I do, or look the way that I think they should, or live the way I think they should—why they wouldn't have a problem at all!" I had to adjust my attitude and change that type of mentality.

I had no compassion for my former husband when he was drunk. It must have been difficult for me to feel any other way when I didn't understand that alcoholism was indeed a disease, especially so when he was constantly degrading me and there was so much negativity. The disease certainly took its toll on our family, including our two precious daughters. Reproaches and tears only made matters worse. I couldn't have compassion for him when I had so many expectations, based on my needs and wants for our life. Unfulfilled expectations became resentments and anger; what an unhappy life that led all of us to live.

One of the most effective types of encouragement and understanding, in my humble opinion, can be learning to be a good listener. Before working the program, a major character defect of mine was not being a good listener, but I've made great progress in developing a caring, responsive attitude. In trying to be a better listener, I often had to bite my tongue to keep from cutting someone off, adding my own antidote, or finishing his/her sentence. Besides all of this, I was busy in my head, planning what I'd say to them—while they were still speaking!

I now realize that just providing an unbiased ear is one of the kindest, most human things anyone can do for others, regardless of whether or not they consider themselves to be an alcoholic. I don't have to comment all of the time; I don't have to believe everything an alcoholic says (and some others...), and I don't have to offer them any advice. I can simply share my ESH (Experience, Strength, and Hope) and be available for them.

My greatest progress, early in my recovery, was to stop doing what I had always done, which was to build other people up while I put myself down. I set a boundary for myself with the encouragement and support of my sponsor, a credible source. I stopped attempting to encourage and support others until I could learn to do that for myself first.

As I became able to release my resentments against others, and myself, I was able to extend compassion to alcoholics. I could love myself enough to love them also, but I can still hate the disease that almost destroyed both of us in my first marriage. I began to look at them through the eyes of the God *of my understanding* instead of through the old anger and bitterness that I had carried around most of my life.

I learned to offer compassion by letting go of my bitterness and resentment (I still have some that can pop up), but I have come a long way in dealing with the "isms." The way I learned to react to alcoholism had gradually become the way I reacted to every situation in my life. I didn't trust the appearance of anything or anybody, and I jumped to conclusions too readily. With the help of my Power Greater, I think the most important thing for me now is to do loving acts for as many people as I can. Genuine loving acts, like going to meetings, encouraging others, listening to others—especially newcomers—will make me a much better person in the eyes of my God, and to almost all others.

My sponsor told me I could be an example of compassionate understanding to my children, who are grown, to my grandchild, to my neighborhood, in the stores where I shop, anywhere that my actions are in the public eye. Having serenity means that I can use the slogans "Easy does it" *and* "Live and let live" every day, for the rest of my life.

My first husband is the father of my children, and will always play a part in their lives, if not mine. He never did join the A.A. program to try to get sober, and is now in an assisted living environment. I can only pray for him. Attraction, not promotion, is encouraging to any alcoholic in my life, and by my taking care of myself I show him/her that I value myself; *that there is a spiritual solution where no human solution can be found.*

For so many years I lived in the same rut; the feelings of worthlessness, uselessness, self-pity and loathing were everywhere, and with the help of others in the program I learned that I could change my circumstances. We continued to live together for six months after I found Al-Anon, and they suggested that I didn't have to take his abuse—verbal or physical. I didn't have to cover him up when he passed out cold on the floor. I didn't have to try and get him to bed. He chose to get that drunk, and so he was responsible for the consequences. It is a family disease, and those affected by it are just as sick (and sometimes sicker) than the alcoholic. Others in the program taught me how to offer encouragement and not enable, to love and let go, not control and cajole.

Even after we were divorced, I still had contact with my former husband, either by telephone or in person. He would bestow long, demeaning tirades, and not allow me to interrupt, give an explanation, nor depart from him. The best protection I could give myself was usually to not respond, not to react, try to keep my peace within, wait for the storm to pass, and go about my business in some semblance of reasonable manner. I saved my responses, let them settle and become reasonable, and only offered them if a time came up when he was calm and receptive, and my suggestions would then be helpful.

We have many dual members in our meetings (members of both A.A. and Al-Anon). In the beginning, I found I could best encourage them to participate in our meetings, when I stopped judging and started accepting them the way they were. When I used to judge them and start labeling them as *alcoholics,* I could lose compassion and take on a holier than thou attitude. If they grew up with alcoholics, or lived with an alcoholic, they were just as entitled to be in one of my program meetings as I was.

Al-Anon has taught me to focus on myself and to begin to heal from my unhealthy thinking and behavior. As I heal and grow, my attitudes and my actions reflect that positive growth. I no longer feel the need to cause any human being at all to feel *less than* in order for me to feel worthy. This program has taught me that I am worthy, just as I am, and I'm a work in progress; I now treat any active alcoholics in my life with the respect that we all deserve. I've learned to detach with love, which results in a much healthier atmosphere for all concerned.

Working the tools of the program and coming to believe that only a Power Greater Than Myself has the power to sit on the judgment throne has helped me move toward thinking compassionately. I'm convinced now that unto itself, compassion is simply love in action; unconditional love such as my God offers me. It follows acceptance of whatever another person thinks is a challenge to them without taking their personal inventory or judging them. It means responding to another's spiritual needs in appropriate ways. Many times it involves nothing more than being available for the other person to sit with them and just listen.

God made me a very loving, caring person (although there have been times to my own detriment). I could never be contemptuous of a crippled person, for that would be unkind in His eyes; therefore, in carefully taught lessons, my Higher Power changed my self-righteous thoughts to those of love and concern for the alcoholics in my world. (Another small spiritual awakening was completed.)

It's much easier for me now to spontaneously offer anyone encouragement and support, alcoholic or not. It seems to spring from me without any particular effort on my part because I learned by first giving that to myself. I thank my fellow members in the Twelve-Step groups and my Higher Power for that gift.

Working the Twelve Steps also helps me to accept that their Higher Power is guiding the addicted one wherever/whenever they need to go. When I chose to accept that alcoholism is an incurable disease and one that can only be controlled by sobriety and the help of the A.A. program, I began to live my Al-Anon program as enthusiastically as possible. Only then did I begin to move forward in my recovery and a beautiful new way of living.

I had to become aware of my own denial, anxieties, attitudes, and self-will, judging myself in a self-defeating manner, guilt, obsessions, and anger. Alcoholism produced in me a distorted sense of self-righteousness and self-pity; I thought that I was a Saint and he just couldn't recognize that! If I didn't have to drink alcohol to relax, why did he? Today I face the reality of my life as it flows from my Higher Power and I live in the here and now.

The disease of alcoholism is a chronic and progressive disease. This means that it never goes away, and it is never "cured." It is always present and continues to get worse over a long period of time. In fact, even if an alcoholic is sober, the disease progresses, and *that is a scary thought for me at times.* I am now married to a twenty-five year sober alcoholic who tells me "he is only an arm's length away every day from the bottle," but I give it all to God, and I know he also does.

I gave up the halo I had been wearing. I threw away my magic wand that I thought made everything "all better" for my loved ones, but never for myself. I've learned to set good boundaries now that keep the focus on myself. I created time, space, and energy for my own needs, and my emotional health. When I know how to be spiritually balanced and keep centered on my inner Spirit, then I can use the compassion and caring that God gives me, and not let my self-will take over my thoughts and behavior. Most importantly, I don't build up resentments today.

I still feel like a newcomer some days. I could not have found the peace and serenity of this program if I hadn't believed that recovery is a process. Only last week I identified that I was reacting to a mood swing of my sober alcoholic. I was straight back to square one. However, I was able to share my feelings with some other members and was offered insights that helped. The program is one from which we never graduate, and I am ever grateful for that.

With all that is available to me now through Al-Anon—meetings, giving service, the fellowship, sponsorship, and by learning to see my problems from a different perspective—I no longer doubt that alcoholism is a disease. However, it's also a disease where I know there is hope in the program for the family and friends of alcoholics and addicts; physically, mentally and spiritually. The choice is mine and the footwork is mine

# 10

## *Anxieties and Fears*

Before finding Al-Anon, fears and anxieties absolutely consumed me, and they became my Higher Power. I tried to treat them by practicing Mary-my-will-be-done, because that was the only way I could make myself feel emotionally better and "safe." This solution only led to more anxieties, and you'd be correct in thinking that my life must have been miserable. Many times fears prevented me from developing faith in a spiritual source of power greater than any other.

Actually, I discovered in working the Steps that I wasn't aware of how much I had been overwhelmed by fears and anxieties until I did my Fourth Step inventory with the help of a program sponsor and realized that fear had caused many of my difficulties. The Twelve Steps led me to face my fears instead of doing emotional and geographic runaways. I did that by practicing trusting in my Higher Power, one day at a time, and letting Him have one fear at a time.

The sad thing is that most of my fears had nothing to do with my reality—whatever God was putting in front of me at any given moment. My beloved, twenty-five-year-sober husband has taught me that I can start a new day beginning at any moment; I can begin my day over again at any time. That's what I try to do now if I think I am not doing as well as I believe I could/should be doing. If I complain about anything, my program sponsor usually will ask me "Are you using the Steps and Traditions to try to find your solutions Mary, or are you simply running on self-will?" I need reminders like that on a regular basis to keep me grounded and centered in our great program and fellowship. There really are no problems, only things that haven't gone as Mary-Glen expected they would.

Tension and anxiety were part of my every-day living and routine. I heard one time that medical science has established that a prolonged state of fear and worry affects the body so drastically that it sets the stage for almost every type of disease. I believe that in my case, I am a living testimony that theory is true. Most of my married life the active disease dominated and interfered with everything I attempted to do. I never felt physically well, but the doctors were unable to diagnose any health problem. Today, I don't have all of those mysterious maladies I used to suffer from, and I have serenity I've never experienced.

I was only able to reach that state of tranquility when I convinced myself that by working on them alone, I never would be able to conquer my anxieties, so I learned to surrender them to God. That was a tough one for me, because anxieties had become just part of my life. Thoughts even went through my head of "Good grief, what would I have to think about if I didn't have them?" We say in the program, If you pray, why worry? But if you're going to worry anyway, why pray? I realized I must step out in faith with God as my companion, using daily—sometimes moment-to-moment—conscious contact, which I know as prayer now.

Some people working the Steps for the first time think that letting go is difficult. It became easier for me when I finally accepted the fact that God is in charge, and I was tired of the "what ifs and if onlys" in my life. I was always worrying and battling F-E-A-R, which in the program we know as False Evidence Appearing Reality. I find that willingness to share my fears in meetings is an effective way to deal with them—sharing can melt the fear away—or I'll be given new insights to deal with it by other members. I also can ask my God for guidance now, step back, and let it all go. He can transform my fears into something positive.

I found out that I can be scared, but I can overcome that fear by telling myself that I believe He is standing right beside me. People in my nurturing support groups taught me, God knows what you need before you ask Him. That's a good belief for me to follow; nevertheless, there are times I also like to pray—*then I can be sure He does!*

Everyone experiences anxiety in some form or another, even though they use the principles in the Twelve Steps as tools. I find that I can't ignore feelings of fear that arise rather unexpectedly at times. I've been told that even self-confident actors experience anxiety on opening night. I experienced the sensation of my knees knocking, when for the first time in my life I had to serve in a position before over a thousand people; however, I didn't collapse and embarrass myself (besides which, I had a long dress on!) God held me up and I was able to get through that fear of being on stage. I still remind myself to trust Him to do that.

Fear can produce strong "fight and flight" emotions in me. Sometimes they can be great emotions for my welfare and safety; however, at times they can be so overwhelming that they control me, rather than my controlling them. Someone once told me to picture everyone sitting there naked, but that one hadn't worked for me while going through that particular incident. What does work is to keep asking my Higher Power to help me by keeping His arms tightly around me. I've been told that there is nothing wrong with admitting that I'm fearful of a new experience, and that it would be abnormal if I didn't feel fearful. Al-Anon members taught me that simply acknowledging the fear, whatever it may be, gives me power over it, The best way to eliminate any fear is just face it and do whatever I have to. Yes, it works when we work it, but it can take years of practice.

My sponsor drilled into me that my serenity is always more important than someone else's agenda. That I need to continually be aware that I tend to have trouble drawing a boundary line sometimes between where my responsibility stops and someone else's begins. I find if I start my day focused on Step Three and taking care of me first, then the rest of the day can be, as God wants it to be. Then I'm peaceful, and the funny part is that everything gets done without my suffering any stress from rush and anxiety.

A mentor taught me to use positive affirmations in all of my daily actions and behavior. One of those was: Instead of telling myself, "I will not be afraid" to make myself feel better, I should think instead, "I am at peace, prepared for what I have to do, and strong with God's arms around me." That worked for me—when I worked it. Definitely, I will always need my Twelve-Step Family's suggestions because they do help me grow.

I heard an acronym for LIGHT as Letting In God's Higher Truth. I really like that. The further away I get from a source of light, the more the light fades. I think that's the way it is in my program. If I don't go to many meetings, or if I skip them altogether (horrible thought), I could easily lose my serenity and my inner peace, even though it would be temporarily. God is my source of power and light from within, and at times He uses other members to carry His wisdom to me. I absolutely depend on meetings to keep me emotionally healthy. I have always loved—and lived—the old Bible saying, "I am a lamp unto thy feet and a light unto thy path." I follow that light now, unconditionally, because He has led me to true inner peace that nothing in this world can destroy.

The word "Spirit" is originally from a word meaning breath. Breathing air is an absolute necessity if I am to continue to live as a human being on this earth.

We all know that every plant and human being needs air and light. My Power Greater is the source of that air, and is the light I need. With every breath I take, I breathe in God and blow out evil. That spiritual thought is what helped me overcome the habit of hyperventilating caused by my fears and anxieties while living with an active alcoholic.

I hyperventilated so much because of anxieties as a young woman; I even stopped driving on the freeways in Southern California for a long time. I'd take all of the streets to avoid doing that, even though the freeways in Los Angeles began when I was sixteen, and I spent a lot of time with my father learning to drive on them.

I recall one time when I was still gripped by the phobia of driving on the busy freeways—like the Freeway #5 in Los Angeles. We had a sudden Southern California type cloud-burst and I had great difficulty seeing, because the windshield wipers couldn't operate fast enough to allow me to see where I was going. I was horror-stricken and begged God to help me get through it all. Suddenly, as in a miracle, the rain stopped as quickly as it had begun; and there, straight ahead of me was part of a beautiful rainbow. I'm positive that was God sending me a message that day that He is always with me. I slowly began to lose my anxieties about not only traveling busy freeways, but also about many other serious challenges.

I've now discovered the wonder and miracle of prayer and letting go—surrendering all to a Power Greater. I think of fears and anxieties now as merely feelings that I can give to Him. We say in the Twelve-Step program, our Higher Power lets us make U turns. That means I have choices. It's okay to make a mistake or use a different path if it's a better one for me, and I don't have to apologize to anyone for doing that. Today I can avoid using denial of my fears. Instead, they are a signal I've temporarily lost my connection to my source of Power and strength.

As I previously explained, I am a member of the great MacGregor Clan of Scotland and they are proud, courageous people. I was always an extremely shy, timid person. I had absolutely no clue I had inherited their courage until I was led to the Twelve-Step program, and a dual member told me one evening, "I was one gutsy little lady." I responded, "I don't feel that I am," but he insisted that I was.

In retrospect, I agree with him now. I did have a lot of courage, but I was like the Cowardly Lion in the Wizard of Oz who said, "I've had it all along; I just didn't believe it!" One program definition of courage is *the willingness to do the right thing in spite of fear,* but I am aware, nowadays, that *ha*ving a lot of courage doesn't mean I'll not have feelings of fear. Many times my God means those feelings of fear to protect me from harm, but I can surrender them to Him as they arise. I believe now that courage is fear that has been shattered by the unconditional love from my brothers and sisters in A.A. and Al-Anon, and God.

Program teaching is that Al-Anon is not a preventive medicine to allay my fears, but instead gives me a way in which to cope with them as they happen. I am convinced that acceptance itself is a process, and it does not come easily. I am now committed to many different positions in my service work in our fellowship, for I now have serenity and peace that never ceases, and I am no longer overwhelmed with anxieties. Acceptance (as the result of working the steps) does not require me to *resign or admit defeat* when I run into obstacles in my service commitments, but rather allows me to live in the solution, rather than being part of the problem. Today I am able to pray, even though fearful at times, "I have this problem dear God, now what do you want me to do about it?" Once in a while, He tells me in a loud and clear inner voice, "Do nothing—simply wait a while." We call that being "in God's waiting room" in my fellowship. I don't get that answer often, but I can accept it now.

I have a very special, comfort sanctuary in a corner of my home where I receive power, healing, and peace, and I find all of these things in two-way prayer and meditation when I write down my thoughts from God. With the help of a Greater Power than myself, I get to fashion, shape, and choose what kind of life I will have today: a life full of peace and harmony with others. And that is one of the awesome blessings of my Twelve-Step program.

# 11

## *Asking for Help*

I used to hesitate about bothering my Higher Power with what I called, little problems. I've since learned that most of my problems are about the same size to God, whether or not my perspective sees them as big or little. This has made it much easier to trouble Him with my issues, because I don't worry now whether or not they are major enough to give over to Him. I know that He is big enough, loving and kind enough, and always "there" waiting for me to call on Him. This knowledge fills me with comfort and gratitude: two feelings I wasn't aware of before coming to the meetings and starting to live this great program.

Sometimes, someone who acts as if he/she does not need or want help needs it the most. I used to be one of those people. Asking for help is easy today. Not doing so before Al-Anon created a lot of unnecessary sadness for me, and was a negative trait of mine before working the Steps. Because of childhood abuse, I became extremely independent as an adult, and I lived in isolation when I wasn't at my place of employment. How could I ask others to help me when they barely knew me? So I hid behind my well-practiced smile and tried to *do life on my own,* but I kept slipping into a quagmire of self-pity and bitterness.

I used to judge myself unmercifully when I felt helpless and asking for help was one of the most difficult things to do. (Perhaps that stems from when I was a child and was often told by an abusive mother, "Stop crying or I'll give you something to cry about.") I was probably afraid to ask for help for fear it wouldn't be offered to me. I always got a massive explosion from the alcoholic when I requested help, then it would be reluctantly given. Accordingly, I got used to struggling with a lot of things myself, rather than ask for help from him. I had to overcome that reluctance to ask for help from anyone. Through time, I discovered that my friends in the program were there for me when I needed something, like sharing a problem or physically helping me with something. They were all loving, caring people I could trust.

I'm a recovering perfectionist and I wanted everything to be done right according to my impossible standards. I think I became a perfectionist because I kept striving to prove to myself—and everyone else, for that matter—that I'm worthy and that I have a purpose to my life. I felt I had to perform any task by myself so that I'd be sure it was done Mary-my-way. I tried to control almost everything around me in an attempt to create an atmosphere I'd feel comfortable with. All of that was part of living in a fantasy world of my own making. I had suffered from feelings of rejection and abandonment most of my life, and my attitude was, "I can do it myself, thank-you." I only became able to reach out for help from all others in the program when I was no longer afraid of being rejected. In the beginning, I had to learn to accept "no" as an answer from someone, and yet be able to think of him or her as a good program friend that simply had no solution to offer me, or who was unable to physically help me at the moment.

When I finally admitted that I didn't have the answers for anyone—even myself, on occasion—only then was I ready to look to God for help. He can do for me what I cannot do for myself. In the Twelve-Step program, we all have the desire to help each other and share our burdens; however, each person has to work his/her program to the best of their ability. Only the person himself/herself can heal their wounds, and that is only with the help of a Higher Power. If I think someone needs help and they might be reluctant to ask for it (as I used to be), I can ask them, "How can I help you?" or "Is there something I can do for you?" I still have to leave the responsibility for whatever needs to be done with the person who has the problem. Otherwise, it's a matter of M.Y.O.B.

Today, I know I need my Power Greater to guide me with His wisdom, one day at a time. I need others so they can help me; I need others so I can help them. Alone—I am not enough. My loving program family is always there for me; they're just waiting to be asked, and I never have to feel alone and isolated again—ever! That is absolutely one of our program miracles for me.

# 12

## *Attitudes*

My experiences in life helped develop the person I became, before changing myself with the help of the Twelve Steps and actualizing them in all of my relationships. I have changed my attitude by altering my thinking, and I am still in the process of developing an attitude of forgiveness and tolerance of others.

I used to feel uncomfortable around someone who continually "bragged" or "boasted" in an attempt to show others that he/she was more superior in knowledge. I had little tolerance for that type of communication since it made me feel as if it were a "put down" of others (even if it's quite subtly done), and, I felt, simply to make him/her feel good about themselves. I am still inclined to jump to someone's defense, if someone is trying to chop him or her down. Today, I try to see the offender doing that in a different light—not from a judgmental view—but with a different attitude, and that is through the eyes of God. I think of them now as being where I was in the beginning of my work on the Steps. Simply not knowing my true inner self enough to be honest and open about who I am, where I am, and not feeling comfortable about letting that true self be known.

Now I question myself, did I ever use that type of 'braggadocio' in an attempt to cover up a low self-esteem and feelings of insecurity? Thank God for my support family that showed me love, no matter how I sounded in meetings. Slowly, I learned to find more meaningful ways to share and to grow in self-approval and confidence.

I'm convinced now that my attitude is definitely something of which I alone am in control, regardless of how others around me choose to behave in the moment. I choose to begin my day by thanking God for my gifts of good physical, emotional, and spiritual health, and ask Him to guide me in all I think, say, or do.

I believe now that I create whatever atmosphere I want to have around me, with the help of a Power Greater Than Myself. At the beginning of my journey I was told by a mentor, "If you believe you *can* and believe it strongly enough, you'll be amazed at what you can do!" I agree with her 100% today. I am amazed at how far I've come and everything I've accomplished along the way, but it has only come with a lot of help from my creator and an attitude of belief in Him.

When I went through the process of committing my life and my will to the care of God, *as I understand Him,* I was told by other members, "That doesn't mean you get to sit around waiting for the miracles to happen. There are steps and footwork that you must do in order for His will to be carried out." As my Higher Power only wants what is best for me, that meant I had to have a huge "attitude adjustment." I had to learn to accept myself just as I am. There are days that can be difficult, but once I have acceptance, the action usually becomes clearer for me. The three "A's": "Awareness, Acceptance, and Action" work miraculously for me.

Sometimes the action can be something as simple as just walking away when I feel it's not the right time or place for me to be there. Or it can be simply taking a moral inventory of myself and being honest about my own undesirable human failings and attitudes. My program teaches me now that action makes the difference between merely wishing my life would be different, and making those wishes come true.

By continuously trying to control an active alcoholic, I became controlled by him; I let him have power over me. One of the few things I know today that I can control is my own attitude. My sponsor taught me I could only change what I think, say, or do. I have a choice today to cultivate a positive outlook and attitude, and I alone can do that. I can surround myself with people, places, and things that bring me happiness, or I can let myself drown in my own negativity.

Today I choose to include laughter in my daily life. With the help of others in my program, I discovered that when I found the ability to laugh at myself, I was indeed on my way to finding true tranquility. By listening to others share their wisdom, I know now that if I am having disagreements in any relationship, I shouldn't dredge up all of the wrongdoings of that person from the past. I have to stay in the present moment. That program principle alone makes my life more pleasurable. I don't want to be forced to look at past bad memories of my own inappropriate behavior; so why should I subject them to that?

I don't eat junk food if I expect to have good health in my body; therefore, I don't put negative thinking into my soul either, because that negative thinking acts as junk food for my soul. That would surely destroy my spiritual health. By having only positive thoughts about myself, I am enabling my soul to receive positive nourishment from a Higher Power.

I find the best way to change any bad attitude I fall into is to go to a place of love; physically, by finding some loving arms, but if they're not available, then I seek a spiritual place of love. I go inward to my special sanctuary, have a "chat" with God, and just let His love take over my being. I remember all the love that has been given to me by other members, and I fill myself with all of the love I possibly can; until there's no room for anything else. Only then *does my attitude change to one of love itself.* I like myself better, and I hope those around me do also. If I am to have meaningful relationships and discover my own true self-worth, I must look for opportunities to enlighten others who are new to our program principles. I can only do that by keeping a cheerful, positive attitude.

I wish I didn't have occasional attitude (and behavior) problems, but I wouldn't be a human being if I didn't have faults. I reluctantly admitted them in my Fifth Step because I was ashamed of them. Now I don't justify or rationalize; I can just acknowledge them and work on changing them.

I am free now to choose my attitude under any circumstances that flow my way, to choose my own way of living with the help of other Twelve-Step members. When I radiate spiritual compassion and love, I add value and meaning to my own life, and people are drawn to me. Coming from a lifetime of almost complete isolation with an actively drinking alcoholic, that is meaningful to me.

Changing my attitudes with the help of the Twelve-Step program means I can set boundaries, I have choices, and I can get out of my own way. By doing that, I'm surrendering any self-pity, misery, and bitter thoughts to a Divine Power. When I live these principles of the program, I am taking responsibility for my heart and soul, and for my welfare. Conscious contact with God keeps me right where I am supposed to be each moment, and doing what He wants me to be doing. These principles are so clearly defined for me in the Twelve Steps and they seem so simple to follow, but it has taken me many years to change my former way of seeing life as it could be instead of "it is what it is." I can only change myself, and life truly is: It all begins with me and ends with whatever my Power Greater has planned "Just for today."

There are occasions when my sober alcoholic husband is in somewhat of an R.I.D. mood (Restless, Irritable, and Discontented, they call it in A.A.) Early in our relationship I emotionalized that as being something about me—something

I'd done. After many years of discovering the joy of keeping the focus on my *own* inner being, I'm able to detach from any depression he may have at the moment.

I've developed acceptance and surrender to the point now that I can remind myself that I am not *always* sweet and patient myself. His unhappy moods and tone of voice remind *me* to watch my *own* body language, manner of speaking, and attitudes.

Attitudes of self-will and self-righteousness used to get in my way. When I began to use the tools of the program and let God's will guide me instead of my own distorted thinking, only then did I begin to know peace of mind.

# 13

## *Boundaries*

Having boundaries was certainly a new concept for me. It was one of the first things I learned; however, I had no idea of what my boundaries were. How could I, when I had no concept of who I was. I had to discover the true Mary-Glen before I could set boundaries.

Self-exploration in the Steps helped me discover how I felt about certain things, other's actions, and situations. I formed definite opinions of what was okay and what was not, because I am responsible for my own wishes, goals, plans, and desires.

Through other members' sharing in meetings about the boundaries they had in place in their own relationships, I gained special insights about my own. I discovered that I should keep things inside the boundaries that will satisfy my own inner Spirit, and keep things outside that will harm me. My sponsor taught me that I'm responsible for: "How I feel, what I want, and what I need," because without knowing those things my "yes" or "no" answers to others have little meaning. I am responsible for my own level of happiness, and no relationship can do that for me. So self-control and being able to assert myself is a very important part of my program boundaries.

I cannot expect to place limits on another person's behavior; since that would only be an illusion on my part. I learned to set limits on how much unacceptable behavior I would tolerate from all others, and for what length of time I would let myself be subjected to his/her actions that offended me. I'm aware now that I do not have to be in situations with people with whom I am not comfortable with their speech and/or behavior. Separating myself from people who are toxic to me is not being inconsiderate; rather, it's being in charge of my own life and protecting it from harm.

If someone verbally attacks me, I don't have to react by being defensive. I cannot change others or make them behave in a proper manner according to my perspectives. They have a right to be whatever way they choose; but I have the choice to remove myself from their performance. I no longer have to compromise my dignity, put myself down to satisfy someone else's ego, or put up with abuse.

I threatened my first husband for many years with divorce, but I didn't back up my boundaries and let him face the consequences. That was simply making idle threats. Fear of being alone kept me in an unhealthy situation with him for far too many years. I found the support I needed in Al-Anon, and discovered that they offered me the unconditional love that I had been longing for most of my life. I found strength, through their help, to finally stand up to my actively drinking alcoholic, and assert myself enough to set the limits I needed for protection against any further harassment from him. I was no longer alone.

I found that boundary setting should begin by my setting them from the "inside out"—on my own distorted thinking and behavior. When I was new to the program, I was afraid of letting people come into my life, because once they were in I didn't know how to set boundaries. They had all the control that way and the power over me. I used to feel that if I said or did something they thought was unpleasant, people would move away from me. (Fear of abandonment and rejection was one of the major issues I had to deal with from my sad past.) Not now because I've been carefully taught that boundaries are not being selfish; I'm simply using self-preservation. I have to constantly keep uppermost in my mind the principle that I am responsible for my own self-care, and whatever it takes to provide for my own happiness.

There came a time when I began to understand that I didn't need to make the other person's point of view my point of view. If I was interested in a healthy friendship with another program member, it was likely that I would need to determine a few insights about what they *expect from me*, and what boundaries they had for themselves. In some cases, drawing a boundary for my benefit is seen as hurting others. Early on, my sponsor told me that when this happens to say something like, "I'm sorry if my taking care of me hurt you; that was not my motive," and "I'm sorry you feel that way." Well, it took me a long time to understand that statement; but I certainly do now.

I no longer have to give that explanation. I can see if I'm taking care of myself when I do my Tenth Step daily examination and inventory, or if maybe I'm slipping into resentment. The resentment only hurts me, and I don't want to go there. My boundaries don't have to agree with anyone else's, and that sets me free from controlling.

I know what I want and don't want. Today, I'll go to any lengths—set many boundaries if I have to—to preserve the dignity, self-confidence, self-respect and individuality that I've worked so diligently to achieve. Nevertheless, I watch to make sure I'm not setting boundaries in order to force my expectations on another person. That is not a healthy attitude for me and only builds up walls—not intimacy. When I know my limits and am true to my own principles I've actualized in the Twelve Steps, and act accordingly; my relationships with others will improve.

No improvement can come for me until I'm consistent in thoughts and action. That means no judging, blaming, excusing, condemning, justifying or rationalizing. If I work the program principles on a daily basis, my actions, attitudes and tone of voice will reflect exactly what my boundaries are. Hopefully, others will see them also.

Boundaries identify where I end and someone else begins; what I own, and they don't, of my life. I am responsible for my own self-care and whatever it takes to provide for my own welfare. A program mentor taught me that boundaries define my inner Spirit and help me guard and maintain it.

My Higher Power allows me to have lessons about helping people and setting boundaries as I help them. I learn where I begin and end. I will always be a helpful and nurturing person and will always have the temptation to help other people; however, I have to work on not losing myself in the process. I need to get rid of any old thinking and behavior patterns.

I grew with the help of the Steps to understand that when spelling out a boundary for someone else, I have to remember to stay kind, gentle, respectful, *but firm*. Boundaries help me create the type of atmosphere I want around me, no matter where I am or whom I'm with. I can make them now, instead of having to build a block wall of isolation around me for protection as I did before the program. That block wall was the only coping tool I knew at that time. I can create a good protective wall now by simply using the appropriate words as boundaries. A very basic one is the word *no*. When I use that word, I am telling others I have a life of my own and I am in control of that life.

Today I know how to protect myself before someone can hurt me, because I was taught by others in my support groups to examine my past behaviors in different situations and what I (alone) could have done to prevent the pain I brought upon myself by not understanding boundaries.

One example of boundaries I discovered is: if someone is pressing me for personal details of my life that I don't want to talk about, I can set a boundary by validating his/her feelings by simply saying, "I appreciate your interest; however, I don't wish to discuss that." Then I can simply change the subject and move on. In the beginning, I felt I was betrayed by trusting two longtime program people by telling them, in trust and confidence, some very private things about my personal life. I later determined that they had manipulated that information from me, so that they could be the first to run it by someone else.

My understanding now is that people who participate in gossip feel inadequate and have a low self-esteem. My sponsor told me when we discussed this that there are a few people, no matter how many years they have been in the program, that can still be "sick." Today, I go by what my inner Spirit tells me when it's okay to trust someone, and I usually don't go wrong.

One thing I do know for sure: is that I want to widen the boundaries of my dreams and goals I've set for myself with the help of the Twelve Steps. I want to go absolutely as far as I can in this lifetime in a spiritual, joyous, free-to-be-me way. With God in charge there are no limits. Anything is possible. I've discovered that doing God's will instead of Mary-my-way sometimes means setting up boundaries and asserting myself instead of asking God to make all others stop being mean, and do things that hurt me. And I can do that nowadays. As I grow in the program, setting boundaries is not so difficult anyway, if I try to surround myself with positive thinking people. With my boundaries I allow less confusion, verbal abuse, and negative energy to enter my life, no matter where I am. Positive others around me most of the time now, makes for positive experiences.

I don't give advice to sponsees regarding the way they should set boundaries because I think they have the right to have their own feelings and establish their own boundaries. They have all of the answers within them, and I have to be careful to let them find those so that they may move in a positive, healthy direction. With the help of their *own* Higher Power, I'm convinced they will. I cannot work their program for them.

I think that "Boundaries," "Detachment," and "Choices" are enmeshed. When I first became aware of and acknowledged my feelings, it was extremely painful. I couldn't do emotional runaways any longer, so I had to face the reality of what life was flowing my way. Program friends taught me that I am responsible for whatever feelings I own, and that I had to stop blaming "him, her, or them" for my emotions. I had to learn to control my own feelings; because if they have power over me, it could lead to my trying to set boundaries in order to manipulate the situation or person. Everyone has a perfect right to live their own life as they see fit. The difference today is that I don't have to try to change how they live or criticize them. I don't live it with them if I don't choose to do that. What others say and do is up to them, *unless it is harmful to me.*

I also learned from others that a true friend would accept and honor my boundaries and be understanding of why I made them. A true friend accepts me as I am, just as I accept him/her as they are. If that's not happening, then perhaps I need to detach from him/her.

By using the principles in our Steps, my boundaries today help identify my inner Spirit and help me protect and guard it. My feelings arise from my heart and soul, so they let me sense if everything is good in a relationship, or if there is a challenge we need to discuss and find a solution satisfactory to both of us.

I now have the courage to tell someone immediately that I don't like something, or I am not comfortable with what they are saying or doing, if it bothers me at all. If I don't deal with it at once and realize later that a boundary needs to be set, then I can do it. Sometimes that can be very difficult, but today I can pray, and the courage will come to say what I have to say. God will give me His wisdom and help when He feels the time is right.

I have the tools of the program and the self-confidence now to sometimes just sit on the issue for awhile until I get that familiar, comfortable feeling about the right thing to do, and that I need to do it for me. That is also the result of remaining closely connected with a Power Greater Than Myself.

# 14

## *Changes, and Accepting Myself As I Am*

By truly appreciating my uniqueness and talents, I came to believe that I could change and become the person God had intended me to be when I came into this world. Lately, I've been reflecting about my life in general, and I am convinced after working the Steps for many years that it isn't just each new phase of my life that means a new beginning for me. Rather, it's whenever God helps me to change any old harmful actions and thinking, He's leading me toward a new way of living, loving, and forgiving. It will always be an ongoing process for my life, maybe even into infinity.

In general, I love change because I enjoy and need variety in my life. I guess its part of my creative side that God blessed me with. I love to travel, make new friends, experience new places, and receive new spiritual enlightenment. Those kinds of changes are chosen changes. The scarier kinds are changes I feel have been thrown upon me without warning—those I'm unable to find a solution for. They're often painful, and I tend to resist them. When I surrender, because of working my program, I've found that these changes also are often for my betterment. As we say in the program: "I have to go with the flow."

I love to think of metaphors as part of my growth and learning. When we lived up in the high country in Southern California part time, I used to be fascinated by the work of the red "fire" ants (of course, not when they bit me because that was very painful). I would watch them digging in for the winter months and creating a new home for themselves. Each small ant would take one infinitesimal grain of sand, and before I knew it, they'd have a little "mountain" circle built around their small hole in the ground. Now to undo that little mountain of theirs, it would have to be done in the same way—only in a reverse manner—and still one grain at a time.

I think that's what I have been doing in my Twelve-Step program for many years now—undoing all of those bad shortcomings I have acquired, one teeny bit at a time, just like the ants and their grain of sand.

I know I cannot go back and undo my past life so it could be as I always fantasized it should/could be. I realize, in my present moments, that each tiny particle of experience contains a lesson for me of what I did wrong and what my part in it all amounted to. Those insights from my God are what gives me the desire, motivation, and willingness, to self-explore and change my distorted thinking and actions toward others.

I began my new Twelve-Step spiritual way of life by determining, with God's help, what the important things are that I treasure and wish to keep; thus began a willingness to change my attitudes and perspectives apropos to what is important to my life and inner peace. Many important things are intangible, as I see them in my life: the beauty of nature, spiritual music, unconditional love, and respect for my loved ones and myself.

I began to understand the difference between being helpful and interfering. I have to remember that another human being also has an infinite and loving Higher Power taking care of him/her. When I step between a loved one and his/her *own* Higher Power, it's as if I were saying, "Let me have a go at it this time, God" and then I am interfering with God's plan for his/her life.

I have forgiven the person I was, I accept myself as I am today, and I love the person I am becoming with the help of this great program because it does all begin with me. Accepting myself means not having to feel I have to be "right," famous, powerful, or rich. It means not having to impress others, but living genuinely, feeling comfortable when asked for help, even if I have to reply: "I don't know" or "Let me think about that and I'll get back to you."

I've heard that the path to inner peace is acceptance of my imperfections and myself *just as I am*—quite a revelation for a recovering perfectionist. But it was true; acknowledging my faults to another human being (my sponsor) in my Step Five and being told that "God still loves you" relieved me of the tremendous burden of guilt I'd been carrying around for such a long time. I felt free to forgive myself and give myself permission to move forward and enjoy the serenity and happiness I was developing.

I lived my whole, married life to the practicing alcoholic as two people: the one dying of unhappiness on the inside, and the one living as my outside self. On my job at the school district, I was the one who always had a smile and "every-thing is great"—a "Pollyanna" attitude. What a phony personality I developed, and became. Most of my life I tried to perform some "remodeling" on my mother and my first husband by trying to change their opinions and behavior, so *I could feel comfortable with them.* That emotionally unhealthy thinking only destroyed the peace and harmony in my life that I was desperately seeking.

Changing and becoming aware of what I need to be responsible for—how I feel, what I want, and what I need—takes lots of time and effort, and lots of sup-port from other members. They taught me that I have to remember that the pro-gram is not a magic potion that will instantly cure my ills, but rather is a pattern for living that will serve me to exactly the degree that I *work it.*

I think most of us need to go to meetings long enough to learn that the other person's problem is not our fault; to learn it's a selfish program of taking care of ourselves. These two principles are a great beginning; however, if I had stopped working the program there, I'd still be at the starting line. The Twelve-Step jour-ney and my Higher Power have taken me to places that I never planned or expected to be; however, they are good places to simply be.

I've gained many valuable insights through others sharing in the meetings, and many of them have improved my life and my relationships, intimate or other-wise. As an ordinary human being trying to live the best way I can, I find that reg-ular self-examination is a matter of survival. I've reached self-acceptance to the point that I no longer think, "If I could only change this or that about myself." Rather, I try to accept and love myself as I am right now because it does all *begin with me.* By accepting myself just as I am, I am able to accept all others just as they are without wanting to try to change them. (Well...most of the time.)

A mentor in the program taught me a prayer that really helps, "Please God, Help me each day to become aware of my weaknesses and strengths so that I may help others instead of possibly harming them with my actions. And please help me to stay humble, for by doing that I will be aware of only your will for my life."

I began to detach from negative comments caused by others' emotions, espe-cially those of anger. I had based my opinions of myself on what others said about me for so long that I had become a complete stranger to myself. I learned to pay attention to my own feelings. First, by working all Twelve Steps with a good sponsor, then by applying the principles in them to my own daily routine. She also taught me to begin this type of detachment by checking my motives, expec-tations, and making myself a priority, after God of course.

I feel the best encouragement and support I give others now is to accept them as they are, as I do myself today, shortcomings and all. I like the old saying, "It is what it is." My younger daughter used to tell me when I'd cry about how "mean" her alcoholic father was, "Well, that's the way he is, Mom." I never understood the true meaning of her statement until I belonged to my Al-Anon Family Groups.

Now sometimes others in the program seek my support and encouragement to help them, without my having to approach them first to try to be helpful and "fix them." I'm constantly amazed at how the program works in its own quiet, miraculous way. I'm now aware that God uses me at times to help others, but it's also for my benefit and growth. I have many more changes that I still want for my life so I can become healthier physically, emotionally, and spiritually, and I am confident that these will come as I continue to work this program. I want to be of lots of service to God and mankind, especially to those suffering from the effects of alcoholism.

I have been in recovery many years now; the longer I stay, the more I may learn. But I can be on a little mini-vacation away from home with Paul, and if I don't have an Al-Anon meeting or two, I can sometimes begin to fall into some unhealthy thinking and feelings. The program works, however, only when I am willing to do what it takes. That will be a lifetime endeavor for me.

Practicing the spiritual principles of the program led me to have an inner peace that is apparent to others when I display loving kindness, compassion, and empathetic joy. Even though life's problems pop up now and then, I know I can still find happiness with the help of others in my fellowship, and "This too shall pass."

Life is continually changing my body, mind, dreams, and spiritual outlook. I have to be willing to accept these changes and adjust to them. There may even be times when I don't like the process, but I can deal with that one moment at a time, and with the assistance of my God.

Getting older doesn't mean I stop enjoying life. I feel there's never enough time in each day to explore new delightful avenues of entertainment. Maybe one day soon I'll even take time from a busy day to enjoy watching television—other than when I'm down with the flu…

# 15

## *Controlling*

In working the Steps, I did a lot of writing, and I became aware of the type of controlling behavior I had exhibited before Al-Anon. Writing it out showed me the many ways in which I had acted and reacted to the active alcoholic. Discovering my own answers to difficult questions helped me comprehend just how very little control I do have over others, and circumstances.

I think I can safely say that most of the women in my program were probably like me in the beginning. If someone showed me something or shared a problem with me, I just had to look to see what I could fix, or to correct in it to make it better than it was. That became just a way of life for me. When I used to try to "fix" something for someone else—without much success, I may add—I probably robbed the other person of the satisfaction and opportunity to experience the self-worthiness that comes with learning to solve his/her own problem. The committee in charge of my head at that time probably thought, "I don't think you are capable of handling your life on your own, so I will step in and do it for you." That was very egotistical, unkind, and unnecessary. It was like trying to do God's job, and I used to do that under the guise of being loving and "helpful." (Our three "M's" also come to mind here: Don't Mother, Manipulate, or Martyr.)

I had to learn to love with my head, as well as with my heart. In other words, I had to learn to stop and think about what would be truly helpful to the other person, not what would lesson my emotional pain at any cost. If my actions are driven by a search for relief from my own pain above everything/everyone else, then I'm going back to the insanity that brought me into Al-Anon in the first place.

A problem is raised when I try to rescue someone from his/her own self-destruction, such as a practicing alcoholic. He/She must be allowed to experience the consequences of their own behavior. I do have self-control, but I have no "others' control." So today, I try to stay out of the way, zip my mouth, and watch my loved ones as they struggle to solve any problems, all without my help. Amazing! I do that now by using the awareness that; they have their *own* Higher Power to rescue them.

I was taught that; God gives only the best to those who leave choices up to Him. To remember that we have five "G's" in the program: "Get off his back, Get out of his way, Get onto yourself, Get to meetings, and Give Him/Her to God." Reflecting on those alone is enough to let me work on surrendering more control to a greater Power.

It has also been suggested to me by others in the program that when I find myself using the words "You *could* or *should*...do so and so," that I need to examine my actions, because those words can be interpreted by others as being controlling behavior on my part. Therefore, I must strive to eliminate *should* and *could* from my vocabulary, at least where it involves others.

Many of my behavior traits were a direct result of circumstances in which I was raised as a child. Deep within me were fearful childhood memories, and I had an inner child always anxious about someone else's anger, criticism, threats, or violence. Consequently, I had to try to control, or change the people, places, and things around me in order to feel safe. I worried constantly about rejection or abandonment, and I could only feel secure by having the illusion of control. As I worked the Steps, I got in touch with memories of childhood hurts, and I began to heal them with the love and help of the God *of my understanding*. I began to spontaneously give and receive unconditional love from others in my support groups.

I also came to believe that if I have no power over others, then conversely they have no power over me. That was quite a revelation, and I was very excited about that one! Another little spiritual awakening completed.

When I ventured out socially with my first husband and he acted like a drunken fool, my self-image suffered, because I was his wife and I felt his behavior was a reflection on me. As a result, I had to try to control him in order to feel good about myself for after all, I was *responsible for him!* Now that I truly love myself, I don't need to try to control anyone else; I know today that what the other person does *is a reflection on him/her, and not me.*

I learned to take only my inventory, and not that of others. I am not responsible for other people's actions, so I don't have to feel guilty and useless when they do not behave according to my expectations. Today I can allow them the dignity of living their own life as they see fit and learn from their own mistakes. I can also allow others the dignity of choosing to behave as they wish, whether or not I like what I see in them. They are doing what I also do best: being themselves.

The program is my special gift from a Higher Power and I try to see things more through His eyes today. I'm more inclined to accept people as they are, by not wanting to fix them or wanting some changes in them to fit my expectations, as I hope they will be that way with me. I believe God plans everything in life, and when I learned to accept that, I found my peace. By giving people room to be themselves, I've found that some people are not as awful as I thought they were. That is the big difference in my life today. My emotional health is not centered or dependent on others; it is centered on my God.

My Higher Power always allows me to have lessons about helping people and setting boundaries as I help. I learn where I begin and end, and where others begin and end. I will always be a helpful and nurturing person and will always have the temptation to help other people; however, I have to work on not losing myself in the process (get rid of any old behavior).

I also have to be careful that I don't allow others to try to control or manipulate me. I don't have to approve of "suggestions" from others that feel wrong for me, no matter how forcefully they are made or who is making them; even if it is my sponsor or a program mentor with twenty years or more experience. I have to follow the wisdom from my own Inner Spirit.

When I think someone is trying to covertly manipulate me now into helping them with a difficult task that I really don't care to become involved in, I have the right to say "No—but thank you for asking me." I need to do what feels right for me, not simply what I think other people want or expect me to do. It's a matter of keeping a balance between keeping an open mind and respecting myself.

I had an interesting revelation one time. I had sympathy for some others about the problems they were having, and felt somewhat guilty that maybe I should be trying to help them. I caught myself in this old behavior of wanting to help others without first being asked by them to do so, and thought about the first thing I learned in the program: the three "C's." I definitely did not cause the situation they found themselves in. I'm painfully aware that I can't control or cure it for them, and then came the revelation: there was a fourth "C." I may not have Caused the problem, but I sure don't want to get involved in and *Contribute* to the problem. I'm learning that it's not an either/or situation. It's not all about me, nor is it all about them. It's about finding and maintaining balance in all of my relationships.

For most of my life I've struggled with responsibility. Being too responsible for things I didn't need to be, and not being responsible enough for the things I should be responsible for, mainly myself. Today, I try to "Keep the focus on me" with the help of God.

I feel it is my responsibility to create and live my life, based upon who I am and who I choose to be. I am responsible for my thoughts, words, and behavior. I am responsible for all of the love, happiness, and peace in my life, but I can only accomplish those with the help of my PGTM. If things get a little confusing for me in close relationships, I still try to keep centered on my desires and needs; otherwise, resentments may creep in. I enjoy taking time out now to keep in touch with myself without feeling guilty, because I know I deserve it

I focus on my life today, and I let my friends and loved ones take care of theirs. My part in life is to remember: I am not a mastermind to solve all problems; only God is. Live the way I wish and allow others to live the way they wish. I could have avoided so much pain and misery in the past if I had just followed the slogan in our program, "Live and let live." Others do not have to do things the way I do, nor do they have to believe the way I do. I am wrong to try to force them to accept my standards for living.

I can only do that by accepting that I am dependent upon a Power, which is great and good beyond anything I ever imagined or understood before the program: A Power that cannot fail. I want to use His help in making all of my decisions. Even though my human brain can't figure out what the outcome will be, I'm confident that whatever happens will be for my ultimate good, and that gives me serenity.

I have three questions I ask myself if I think I am trying to "butt in" to someone else's life and business. Before I get involved in another's dilemma I ask: 1. Are they expecting me to take on their responsibilities? 2. Is someone asking me to do something that he/she is perfectly capable of doing and should/could take care of himself or herself? 3. Am I getting involved in something that will prevent this person from using their self-respect and dignity to handle it their own way? Usually the solution is to "Let Go and Let God" help them handle it, if I honestly answer these questions.

During the forty years I was married to my first husband, I took care of every single thing for him. (The bookkeeping, paying our bills, buying his clothes, I did all of his thinking.) I made all of the final decisions on everything. The only thing I couldn't do was eat for him, stop his drinking, or assume responsibility for his job. When we divorced, he moved three blocks away from me and probably figured he would continue to be my problem, and I would help him. I was happy to do that, of course, for several years. (Probably I did that out of guilt at that time.)

One day, a few years ago, I was leaving for an out of town convention with my new A.A. husband, and I decided to run down to the market at the last minute to pick up a few things for our trip. As I parked my car, a lady was backing her car out into the driving lane and she was honking her horn at a gentleman with his back to us, trying to force him to move out of her way. I told her to hold on a minute because I thought it looked as if there was something wrong with him. I was shocked when I reached him to find out that it was my ex-husband, as I barely recognized him. Clutched tightly in his hand was a market bag with nothing in it but a half-gallon of alcohol and a carton of cigarettes—no food at all. He was extremely disorientated and about ready to fall over, yet he was trying to walk back to his vehicle. It was over 110 degrees in the shade that day, and there was no shade. I think it's possible, that if he had made it back to his truck, he might have died in it from dehydration and heatstroke.

I believe there are no *coincidences* in my life, and I'm sure that God wanted me to help him—just one more time—and He arranged for me to *just happen to be there* at that particular time. I called the paramedics and they told me they wanted information about his next of kin. I told them, "I guess I am, but we're divorced." They gave each other a quizzical look and said, "You are not responsible for him; we need to have his next of kin." (My daughters.) Ta da! That was the wake-up call I'm sure my sponsor had been praying for me for so long: "Guess what, Mary-my-way, you are no longer responsible for him…"

He did survive and spent about a month in the hospital, and then our daughters moved him to an assisted living home in California, close by them. At least he's comfortable and living a fairly decent life. For the first time in my adult life, I was finally *free to be me*. I had been in Al-Anon about four years when that realization and awareness finally dawned on me. I guess you could say I was a slow learner.

Maybe you are like me; I think if I try to make life easier for everyone else in my life, I'll make him/her happy, but I've learned the difficult way that it doesn't work that way. Everything in life, I've learned the hard way. I am like the child that is told not to touch the hot stove, but touches it anyway and finds out that it hurts, so they learn a lesson by being hurt. And I do also. I have to let my loved ones have the respect and dignity of making their own decisions, learning from their mistakes, and let their Higher Power take care of them.

My sponsor used to keep reminding me of our slogans to "Keep it Simple" and "Just for Today." When I relieved myself of the burden of the responsibility of having to solve everyone else's problems, I was more able to follow her suggestions. I am now married to a longtime sober alcoholic. When he goes into a down mood or something is physically hurting him, I have to step out of the way and let God help him. Nothing I do or say will keep him from drinking if he ever wanted to, so I am learning to detach, and I humbly ask my Power Greater to help me do that. He is only "one day away from the bottle" as people say in A.A., and I am only one day away from my old insane behavior, if we don't work our individual Twelve-Step programs. Besides that, when I get to be a 100 (smile) I may have to live in a rest home and be among some grouchy, negative people. If so, I'll need all of the principles of this great program even more then, especially the principles about not controlling others.

Part of my spiritual development in the program is the realization that we are all human beings, except that we do have differences: You are you, and I am I. I cannot be you and you cannot be me. I decided then that, if that is true for you, and me, then I certainly should never push or shove anyone to be more like me! I surrender all control to my Power Greater and just let others be who they think they are.

# 16

## *Decisions*

If you are now in an unhappy marriage or other relationship affected by some-one's addiction, it is suggested in a Twelve-Step program that you wait from six months to one year while attending meetings *before making* any major decisions. Our perceptions of problems often change after we have worked the program for that length of time. We see miracles happening in Twelve-Step relationships, where the spouse, child, or significant other who is caught up in the addiction, will see the change in our attitudes and behavior after we have worked the pro-gram for a few months. This may lead them to be influenced to seek help for themselves, but seldom to please anyone else.

I think making decisions can also be thought of as part of the Twelve-Step principle, "I have choices." Becoming aware that I had choices was an awesome spiritual development for me. My sponsor told me, I was probably never taught I had choices, and that may be the reason I married the first young man, at eigh-teen years old, that proposed to me. At that time I did think he was the *right one* for me, even though I had very seldom dated others. I loved him, however, I'm sure getting away from my mother's hold on me was uppermost in my mind. I can see now that I thought I was being given a great way of doing that by getting married.

I've since learned that I am in control of my own choices that lead to deci-sions, no matter how much I want to blame someone else for causing my prob-lems. I discovered I need to use ownership, self-responsibility, and self-control in making decisions. If I blame someone else for a wrong one, I'm acting like the child who states, "He made me do it!"

In everything I encounter one day at a time, I have to make personal choices for my own contentment or emotional health. In the past, my self-will (Mary-my-way) only created confusion, fear, and hopelessness. When I pray first for God's will to be done and listen for His wisdom, I am at peace with any decision I make. If I get that old familiar knot in my gut feeling, I know what I am thinking about doing is not God's will for me.

When I began working the Steps, I read and pondered a lot about fear and acceptance, with the help of my sponsor. I almost had to let her do my thinking for a while, for the reason that after living so long with alcoholism I was very confused about what would be best for me. It took a long time before I could do any rational thinking or make the appropriate decisions. Thankfully, I'm now being restored to a more sane way of life. What helped me the most was facing reality and accepting life as it happens. I couldn't have figured that out on my own, and today I choose not to do life alone. I'll always need my great Twelve-Step program and fellowship.

I truly know peace now and I live a contented life—by choice. I'm aware now that I didn't know I had many choices and options before coming into the program; I just allowed others to decide what I should be wanting and feeling. After a lifetime of care giving to others and making choices based on what was expected of me, rather than on what I wanted to do or what was best for me, I ended up feeling worthless and had a big empty hole inside. I was drained from living a life of denial because I denied myself each and every day that I lived a life based on lies, false promises, fantasy instead of reality, trying to control others, and trying to please everyone other than myself.

A mentor once shared with me that her sponsor suggested to her, "There are no problems; only challenges waiting for a solution from a Higher Power." I think about that today when I have a difficult time making a decision.

Before the program, fear almost paralyzed me when I faced making a decision, because I was afraid of what I would suffer from any consequences of my choice. It became easier to take risks when I learned to truly "Let Go and Let God." I keep the slogan, "How important is it?" posted on our refrigerator, and it reminds me that I can sometimes reason things out with a trusted program friend or with my sponsor. They can help me see that just maybe, I am making my problem bigger and more difficult than it needs to be.

I used to think it was a disaster to make a mistake, and that alone would lead me to be completely unable to make the simplest decisions. I could take up to half an hour deciding what to wear to work some days, yet I was perfectly eager and willing to tell others exactly how to manage all the details of their lives. I would even interrupt them if they were asking someone else for advice, and they hadn't even asked me for mine! (Now that was insanity.) I'm now aware, I don't know what is best for others; I don't even know what is best for me part of the time.

There is a saying, "Stop, Look, and Listen," and as a child I was taught never to cross the street in traffic without doing that. Using the Steps, I discovered that I could make plans and look forward to living them, but that doesn't always mean life will follow my script, so I learned to go with the flow of life. My program family helped me relieve the fear of making decisions for myself that could be wrong by helping me see that there are lessons I can learn in every risk I take; whether it is right or wrong. I believe now that every decision I make for myself has a purpose.

It has taken me a lifetime to be aware that the world will go around exactly as it is supposed to, without any effort on my part, and if I do make mistakes I'll be given the Grace to dust myself off and start all over again. Only through conscious daily contact with my Power Greater Than Myself will I find guidance and wisdom to make meaningful decisions.

By facing the reality of "what is," instead of doing a runaway to avoid challenges that had to be resolved, I began to make much wiser decisions that could help me make progress in my new life. Writing about decisions helped me immensely; as a matter of fact, all of my writing helps me—period. I would never be where I am today in my program without the benefits that writing my thoughts has brought me, as well as writing down the wisdom I receive from a Higher Power. Before making a decision, my sponsor would have me write about "What do I hope to accomplish?" "How will I go about getting there?" and "Can I picture myself already living whatever it is that I hope to accomplish?" Today I can do these things, and after a consultation with my Power Greater, I can make the proper decisions for my best welfare and possibly benefit some others.

Other Al-Anons convinced me that I was the only one responsible for my welfare, and after a few years I began to set goals and dreams for myself. I made wise choices and decisions, based on lots of prayer to my Higher Power, asking Him to lead me in a good direction. When I lived with an actively drinking alcoholic, at times it seemed a lot easier to allow an unacceptable situation to continue, rather than actually make a decision to do something about it. Today, the program gives me the tools to decide what is acceptable and what is not, and to set the necessary boundaries, based on those decisions.

Decisions, boundaries, and choices for my own welfare are priorities for me in the new life I have been given, and I thank my God every day for helping me be aware of that spiritual enlightenment.

# 17

## *Detachment with Love*

Before working the Twelve Steps, I thought I was an expert on detachment. The problem was, my only method of detachment at that time was from my own "self." I concentrated on my actively drinking alcoholic husband for a lifetime, and all others, as well. I obsessed so much about them that I lost touch with the real me, myself, and I, and had no sense of self-identity. Today I can let others' Higher Power take care of them (good or bad) and I have peace in my life. I use all of that extra precious time that I now have to really relax and enjoy whatever God sends my way.

There are a few program insights on this topic that helped me begin a better way to live. We talk a lot about the three "A's" in my Groups: "Awareness, Acceptance, and Action." That was one of the first challenges thrown out to me by my sponsor as she told me to look up the three "A's" in our literature and write about them. I like the saying, "Even a step backward is progress." In the beginning of my journey, my God always gave me awareness before I could have acceptance and take some action, and that helped me face reality.

I learned the art of placating at a very early age. I thought it was my job to keep peace in my family, and placating was one of my tools. *Detach* is defined as: "to separate—especially from a larger mass, and usually without violence or damage, or to disengage or withdraw." Now detachment means to me that I don't have to take on the other person's issues; I can separate myself from others and let their problems be simply their problems.

Detachment does not mean to escape into fantasy, as I did before the program. I instilled in my daughters the spiritual moral values I had formed by studying and reading the Bible in the Scottish public schools. Both daughters are exceptionally loving and caring and have a very close bond with each other, and with me. They were able to recognize and accept their father's faults as: "He is what he is, Mother," but I couldn't come to acceptance with that.

I wanted him to be my ideal of a companion, lover, and husband; therefore, I tried to change him, mold him, and remake him into that role. Instead, he remained the mean, verbally abusive person he had become because of his childhood experiences and his alcoholism. That goal to have a loving, understanding companion became my plan and fixation, except he never could live up to my expectations of how he could/should be. He wasn't willing to try to change the things he did that hurt me emotionally, and sometimes he caused me physical harm, nor would he try to address his alcohol consumption.

My only detachment left was the option of choosing legal separation, followed later by a divorce. Those remained my only choices. I first filed for a legal separation, because I had no intentions of remarrying. However, the family assured me that divorce was necessary for my protection, in case he should injure someone or run up excessive charge account amounts because of his excessive, compulsive gambling.

Incase you feel at this point, that most people in a Twelve-Step program end up in divorce, I would hasten to add something here. We have a lot of miracles in AA and Al-Anon, where people are divorced for several years, and are then reunited because working both programs together helps their relationship. And, there are many Al-Anons who try to stay with their actively drinking alcoholic or other addiction, and the Twelve-Step way of life really helps them do that. I sincerely hope that will be your experience.

Others in my program pointed out to me that in detaching with love, I have to acknowledge, and be aware that I do have choices. I have to allow others the dignity and respect to live their lives as they see fit and learn through their own mistakes; as long as they do not harm me in the process. Detachment with love means I can accept a person, and even love them, but I can allow them to own their own feelings, thoughts, and actions. And all of that is all based on faith in a Higher Power who will work things out for the best of everyone concerned.

Detachment is not a lack of caring. I feel it is self-preservation, for me and for those others in the Twelve-Step program who care about a loved one (whether or not he/she is an alcoholic and/or lives with us), and the one I should love first and foremost is myself. As major airlines advise us: "Take care of your own oxygen mask first or you won't be able to help your children or anyone else for that matter."

Trying to detach in my earlier days of recovery was confusing, to say the least. I didn't know what I was doing, why I was doing it, or how to do it. I read a lot about it, and by the sharing of others, I realized how important it was to my sanity. At first I thought I was just supposed to shut off my emotions and ignore my feelings. But hadn't I been trying to do that all along—just numb myself—so I didn't feel the pain of my husband's words and behaviors?

The problem is, I did undergo feelings more than I realized, and instead of recognizing them and accepting them, I reacted to them in ways I shouldn't have. I couldn't feel comfortable about the way I behaved, and yet I would get even angrier with him. I continued our arguments in my head, even when he wasn't there! What a waste of my time and energy that was. We have a saying: "When I got busy, I got better." Not detaching made for some really great house cleaning sessions, but I sure didn't feel any better about the challenges with him, or with myself.

Initially, detachment for me was literal: Get out of the area, walk away and not be present for the hook that wanted to grab me into the problem. With the help of other program members, I realized that I could care deeply about what was going on, without having to fix it or control it, or even get in it enough to muddle the issue with my own "helpful" opinions that no one asked for in the first place! That gave me a great perspective, and I was then able to see that the other person was merely acting out, as we in the program describe it, the "isms" of their disease. Their opinions, thoughts, and actions are no more valid than mine; they simply belong to them, and mine are equally valid and belong to me.

As my faith in the God *of my understanding* has grown, so has my ability to detach with love. At first, practicing detachment was with anger, and that was okay, because it taught me the beginnings of what detachment felt like—sort of like learning to ride a bicycle using training wheels. At first I worried that detaching meant that I didn't care and that what I may be doing was pushing aside all of my feelings. I had to work through all of that with a sponsor in order to be able to truly detach, and now I'm aware that "Live and Let Live" is the most loving thing I can do for another adult, and for myself. I think I finally found part of the "it" I'd been trying to find in the program.

My ex-husband moved about three blocks from where I was living after we were divorced. I allowed him to help me with handyman jobs at my new residence where I lived by myself. Looking back, I can see how sick that behavior was; it only gave him more reasons to see me and heap verbal abuse on me under the guise of "helping me." Oh, yes, people can be "friends" after a divorce, but not if one of them is still actively drinking and is controlled by the disease; and not much else.

I just didn't "get it"—that "it" we are always looking for in the beginning of working the Twelve Steps. Eventually, by working the steps, I could interact with him but detach from engaging in unhealthy behavior. If he shouted, I stayed calm. If he blamed and finger-pointed at me, I did not have to retaliate. I heard a good saying about this type of detachment; it was: "There is no tug-of-war if I don't pick up my end of the rope, because *you can't push* a rope!"

That went on for about three years until I met my beloved sober alcoholic I am now married to. Early in our relationship, we were discussing my problems with my ex-husband and he pointed out to me, "You are divorced. It's over—final! You need to think about why you allow yourself to get involved with him at all, if you don't want to." I had another spiritual awakening and decided, yes, I was just allowing that behavior to continue out of guilt about leaving him. It was time to think only about myself, which is what the people in the program had been telling me for many years.

Detachment can indeed be difficult to understand, and especially to put into action. I have noticed in the program that the concept of letting go, or detaching from an active alcoholic—or anyone else for that matter—can be confusing in the beginning to a lot of people; and it is often "misinterpreted." Some members prefer to think of it as releasing with love, because those words have the connotation of more warmth, caring without possessing, being concerned without dominating, and not trying to control another.

I can see today that my efforts in studying and then applying detachment in all of my relationships were well worth all of my initial doubts and perseverance. Learning to detach is one of the best gifts I myself have been given, and my family and close friends benefit from it, also. I know I couldn't have learned how to detach without all the mentors I had along the way who validated my feelings by saying: "Yes, that was detaching;" "Yes, you are right where you belong;" "Yes, others don't accept it with open arms when you first practice it—they may not like it at all;" and "Keep coming back."

"Don't Even Think About Changing Him" is one of our acronyms for "detach." Detachment (also known as "Mind Your Own Business" in Al-Anon), means having clarity on what is my business and what is not; and staying clear of confusion about what is my responsibility or not. Sometimes I need a sponsor or mentor to help me straighten out the difference and keep a happy balance in my thinking. I have enough problems of my own to worry about, and that is not being selfish. Detachment can be from the person I myself used to be—by not reacting. I no longer blame others for my suffering or unhappiness, for it all begins with me. Our Slogan, "First Things First," now means: take care of Mary before trying to take care of the welfare of others.

There are other ways in the program to use the three "C's." They form three questions I can ask myself:

• Am I trying to "cause" someone to act in a certain way?

• Am I trying to "control" the situation and force the situation as I see best?

• Am I trying to "cure" someone's inappropriate behavior?

And, I have a choice to "Let Go and Let God" take care of them.

I constantly used emotional and physical runaways before the program. I came to believe much later in life that there are no "evil, mean" people as I used to feel there were, only some emotionally sick people. Sometimes their meanness, as I see it, is simply *a cry for help and love; and I can pray for healing for them.* If I do encounter someone I think might truly be an evil, mean one, in my eyes at least, I can choose to stay away from that person or persons; detach, and not have them in my life. I can give them up to God.

Detachment also means living the way I want to and allowing others to live the way they want to. I could have avoided so much pain and misery for myself if I had just followed this simple principle. Other people do not have to do things the way I do, nor do they have to believe the way I do, and it is not appropriate to try to dominate them or coerce them to accept my values. This also works in reverse for me, for if someone takes a suggestion of mine as criticism or offensive, that's not my problem; it's his/hers. I can keep my serenity just by being sure in my heart and soul that I was not being unreasonably critical of others; that I was only protecting my own peace of mind when I made the suggestion.

Many times, "hands off" is good to think of as an attitude of detachment, however, in many situations it can become an excuse for me for not taking appropriate action; for being passive, or for being accepting when I should be changing. Only more years in the program and working on the Steps will show me the difference and help me keep a happy balance in everything I do. My God is slowly helping me get there.

I still have to remind myself that just because someone else is having a bad day doesn't mean *I have to have one.* Allowing myself to be dragged along with, and into, another person's negativity is not helpful to anyone. I have to stop, think, and ask myself if I can do anything to help this other person? In many instances, the best thing I can do is to simply listen. I can be a good listener to someone with fears, but I can't change those fears or make them go away. All I can offer them is my own experience, hope, and wisdom from a Higher Power.

The first time I was actually able to detach from my active alcoholic was after we divorced and he needed a ride somewhere. When I arrived at his apartment, he came out to greet me and started spouting off some expectation he had of me that *he* felt I had not carried out. My first impulse, the old natural reactive way, would have been to defend myself. But other members had been working on me, and I could hear their words chanting through my head: "Those are *his* expectations, *his* feelings, *his* reactions, and *his* choice of verbally abusive words." Only a short time before this happened, they had suggested to me that *I didn't have to react to them as if they were mine to own or defend in the first place.*

That particular day, I remember I remained calm, said a prayer, and asked myself, "Do I really want to match his insanity, or do I want to simply leave him with it, with no one there to yell at?" Instead of reacting with harsh words meant to hurt him in return, I was able to tell myself, "This is not mine to own," and to tell him "I'm leaving now until you're able to communicate in a reasonable manner," then I jumped in the car and sped off! I was so proud of the way I had handled the situation that I just had to "share and tell" it all with my home group that evening; and they all applauded! That was a great milestone in my recovery; I had asserted myself and taken a big leap forward, with their help. My support group family holds me up in place and makes sure I keep my feeling of contentment. I will always need them.

There is a difference between taking care of a dependent child and feeling responsible for an adult child who refuses to grow up and accept his own responsibilities, and that applied to my first husband. Detachment doesn't mean that I don't care; it means that I don't let someone/something affect my daily life. I can care about someone (alcoholic or not) without being affected by his/her criticism. I can allow him/her to face the consequences of his/her actions. His actions are a reflection of him, not of me. It takes endless hours of practice of principles of the program in order to enjoy healthy detachment from the behavior of others that is unacceptable to me.

I also determined that if I detached my emotions from the opinions, criticism, judgment, and attitudes, of negative thinking others, it helped me find healthier ways of looking at reality. So detachment, in my mind now, is also withdrawing in a good way from the feelings of others. Detaching with love means I no longer have to be enmeshed in other's challenges or their addictions. I can let those I love be who they are without any interference from me, and I can say, "I love you and I'm always here for you if you need me, however, these are my boundaries." (I think that is what we mean when we say in our Twelve-Step fellowship: we give *encouragement* to the alcoholic.)

During that first marriage, I used to get my own twenty-four hours off to a great start by walking early in the morning around the neighborhood, taking time to admire the beautiful landscaped antique homes, and the nearby older college buildings. I'd come home again and find him in a bad mood, and any feelings of euphoria I had accumulated would immediately self-destruct. It wasn't until much later in Al-Anon, that I realized he probably had a horrible hangover every morning; however, I didn't know then what I now know—that I could detach from his emotions and stay in charge of my own life.

Most of my life, scolding, nagging, and criticizing others—trying to change them—led me nowhere. Today I have turned my life and will over to a Higher Power, whom I only know by the name of God. Sometimes I picture my God as a man (especially the picture of God as a shepherd holding a little lamb; I love that one), and then there are times when I think of Him as a woman, when I am really hurting and revert to my little inner child again. I visualize my grandmother in her old-fashioned nightgown, in her great big poster bed, and I just climb in with her and hide from those mean, nasty others that are bothering me. Thanks to this great program, I am surrounded by positive people now, and I don't have to use that one very often.

Detachment is something I have to practice daily, at times even hourly, or often by the minute. Frequently, detachment seems to occur automatically, and occasionally I have to consciously work at it. Prayer and meditation always seem to help in challenges involving others, as also does talking things over with other members.

It was tough for me to learn that I can actually do more harm than good by disrupting the natural flow of events. My interference can postpone lessons that can't be easily learned any other way by my loved ones or myself. I am not doing anyone a favor if I get in the way of natural consequences. It seemed to me that the lessons kept getting more complex to cope with, but with the help of Al-Anon, I finally grew enough that I know how to survive the difficult times. I do put a lot of effort these days into minding my own business, and life is becoming less stressful.

Detachment, as used in the fellowship, mainly means for me that now I am recovering from the devastating affects that resulted from living with an active alcoholic. It's helping me become more objective and realistic with circumstances in my life, as well as the lives of my loved ones. This allows me to make more mature decisions.

Detachment with love means now that I can let those I love find their own answers, while I step back into God's waiting room. We have a program Acronym for worry that can also help me detach, "When Others' Recovery Replaces Yours."

Detachment works best when I remember that it is not just a tool of the program I use when a challenge seems to require it, but a solid principle I need to weave into and use in my daily relationships, be they intimate or otherwise. Living a good life through my Higher Power of God, for God, and from God, is a full time job, and I need every program tool I can find in my Twelve-Step work.

I'm certain that the foundation for all of this action has to be humility. I can't detach if I think I have the answers and know what is exactly right for the person from whom I should be detaching. I am trying to play "God" to them by thinking I know what they need and what path they could or should be taking. I can't even fix my own life without the help of my God; therefore, I keep practicing more and more humility. This is how I detach, when I need to, and keep my deep feelings of complete contentment and peace now.

# 18

## *Developing a Closer Relationship with My Higher Power*

I believe there's a special Spirit, generally understood as being a Higher Power in Twelve-Step philosophy, that moves through our meetings and one another. To my mind, a feeling of spiritual healing that we can see, hear, and feel in our groups when we are gathered together. That Spirit turned my life around in a new direction, and a new way of thinking and behaving. I formed a spiritual connection with my religious God that brought me a great sense of peace and acceptance.

When I am able to separate my spiritual thinking from the doctrines and dogma of my religious faith, the spirituality of the program and my religion fit like "hand in glove." Being in the spiritual twilight of my journey on this earth, I need both my church and my great Twelve-Step fellowship. A lot of the lessons I learned as a child in Sunday school are the same basic philosophies as those in the program, particularly the principles that those are based on, "I have a Power Greater Than Myself," and "Love one another."

I was always searching for the answers to the big mystery of life when I was young, curious about my Spirit's origin. I wonder, now, was it by asking God to show me His face—proof that he really existed—that I invited Him into my life? Did that lead to the beginning of my journey toward my spirituality as it is today? I think, possibly, my curiosity and hunger for something more inspired me to keep looking for fresh insights about God. But I believe now that each one of us in a Twelve-Step Program has a spiritual experience leading us to find a Power

Greater in a different, unique manner, and what works for me may not work for you.

At the beginning of my Twelve-Step journey, when I questioned the process of turning over my entire life and will to God, I was told to "just keep going, and act as if," and eventually I'd see evidence that God could do for me what I could not do for myself." I thought, "Okay, I think I can do that!" (We also have a program saying: "Fake it till you make it," but I didn't care for that one; as in my mind, it had a connotation of lying.) I simply acted as if I had turned my will and life over to Him. Amazing things happened; life started getting so much easier to cope with. When I'd hit a hazard in the road, I just acted as if God were already removing it. Or, He'd post little signs leading me in the proper direction.

One day I realized that I was no longer acting as if—I really was letting His will be done, and I had finally resigned as Assistant Manager of the Universe. I had never been qualified or hired for that job anyway; I just forced my way into thinking of myself in that capacity.

I disagree with those who feel they have a partnership with God; however, I believe they have a right to believe that way. I think of partners being equal (as in a business venture), and I certainly do not consider myself "equal" to the God of my choosing. I realize that the word partner can also mean a special relationship. Nonetheless, I never want to feel so self-satisfied and complacent in my relationship with God that I forget that I am dealing with a Supreme, Supernatural Being. No matter how secure my relationship with Him, I feel I must never forget to praise, honor, *and respect His authority.*

Because of a feeling of a lack of love and affection, first from my mother, and then an active alcoholic husband, I think I developed a yearning, then came the willingness, to seek within for something greater and more powerful to fill my spiritual needs. I've learned that it's well known by psychologists that children who are abused have no problem experiencing comfort, love, and a safe feeling through the intervention of a Divine presence that *only they themselves can see and actualize.*

I'm positive that was my experience as a child, because I can remember having a very loving Father in heaven. Notwithstanding, as an adult I had to develop an open, uncluttered, willing mind, and persevere in prayer practice before I could experience that Divine presence again. I'm sure I never intentionally ignored God; I just felt "Mary-my-way" was best done alone!

I don't remember my first sponsor using the name of God for her Higher Power; at least at that time, it seemed to me she shared more about universal energy. I couldn't think about the God *of my understanding* as universal energy, because those words had a connotation for me that it left Him hanging way out there in space somewhere in the universe, and He would be unreachable if I thought about Him as simply "energy."

I've had many spiritual awakenings as they are described in our Twelve-Steps, and one of those was finally realizing that God is not out there in the universe somewhere. He is not merely a spiritual phenomenon nor is he simply energy. He is a *Divine Spirit that lies within my own soul and body.*

I need an image in my mind of a Power Greater Than Myself, something tangible, that my soul can cling to. I have a beautiful picture, well known and loved, depicting the Son of God *(as I understand Him)* holding a baby white lamb in His arms that appears to be so helpless and dependent upon Him. It has helped me think of myself as that lamb being carried in God's arms, while He guides and comforts me with unconditional love. I fully experience that love now; thanks to each and every one in both of our programs.

Finally, I came to acceptance with my own feelings about the expression universal energy that some others use. I believe today that there *is* some type of energy from a Higher Power, which I can't define, yet acts as a spiritual magnet. I am slowly drawn toward other spiritually fulfilled people, just as they are attracted to me, and I think everyone who crosses my path is part of God's plan for my life. In this way, I look at that spiritual energy today as God's unconditional *love for everyone.* When I found my Twelve-Step Support Group, I knew I would never have to feel alone again. Each and every one is very special to me.

I live in a city with lots of gaming, and we have an analogy we use sometimes in our groups: "I don't deal life's cards—only a Higher Power does." It's also true that I have a choice about those that I wish to keep, and those I choose to throw away. I've discovered that I can find spiritual solutions to release any fear I may have by replacing it with trust and love. I 'm convinced now that I don't have to understand how God works in my life; I simply believe that *He will,* and others in the program help reinforce that belief.

I began to keep an open mind and be aware that life-changing help can come in many forms and voices. I practiced this belief and found I could trust that I would be guided, and I could let God be in charge. The more I admitted my powerlessness and surrendered the challenges I could not resolve, the more emotionally stronger I became. I have a choice of struggling with life by myself, or trusting in God. Trusting in Him helps me believe I am cared for—a much easier path for me to travel.

"Letting Go" doesn't mean I ignore problems or pretend they aren't happening now; that would be a slip into old behavior of not facing up to reality. God wants me to be happy, joyous, and free, but I still have to do the footwork, so I set my priorities one day at a time and let Him take care of the rest. I do that by taking one Step at a time, moving in one direction at a time, and doing one thing at a time.

I have always felt that God loved me; He just wouldn't give me what I used to ask Him for! Although I will add, I never have asked Him for material things; I am not a gambler, so I don't ask Him to let me win a big lottery. But I am positive the difference in our relationship now is that He is my guide, my helper, and the most important of all, He is my counselor. When I share my feelings with Him in prayer, I do so with complete humility, and I am continually letting go of my self-will, stubbornness, ego, and judgmental attitudes.

I'm convinced today my prayers go directly to Him, the Omnipotent One. How can I be confident He is receiving them? Well, I believe that one way is by paying attention to regular answers that I receive to my particular prayers, and I will add—in His time, not mine. Before working the Steps, I never thought of it that way; I just took it for granted that *"Mary-my-way-be-done"* had arranged it *all*. Now I try not to give God directions, but simply ask for His help in all I think, say, or do, each day; however, I do make sure I quickly add, "Thy Will Be Done."

I heard somewhere that paying attention to yourself is not self-centered or selfish, but it's an awareness of how we relate to others and relationships. I am learning to let go of the hurt child of the past, and I have to keep doing that process if I want to have peace and harmony in my life today. I've also learned to look for God and His work in everyday happenings; and guess what? He's always there! I'm convinced I never would have found my Twelve-Step program or all of the special people in it that He used to save my life, but for His intervention.

By working the Steps, I have faith now that God has to be my number one priority; after that, I keep the focus on me. I believe now that He wrote the play, His big plan for my life, from my humble beginning on this earth and on into infinity. I can look back now and see that play being enacted at various stages of my life. God's play reveals itself as I live it each moment, and only He knows what the next scene will bring each day. My job is to keep healthy, emotionally and physically, so that I may play the role that He assigns me each day, and to take whatever action He shows me must be done. I can only do that by going to my inner sanctuary on a daily basis—sometimes hourly—and checking in with my Higher Power; and I do that in two-way prayer.

The private time and space I devote to God early in the morning is my time to reflect upon His Word and be in close union with Him. That is how I get my focus for the day; i.e. to keep Him as the center of my life. I don't have to feel guilty, though, if I'm unable to take this special time because of another early morning commitment to my service work or others. I choose and use each precious twenty-four hours to suit my particular needs. By keeping God centered in my own spiritual, emotional, and physical needs, I know I'll have a wonderful day.

My wants and needs have greatly changed by daily utilizing the principles of the Twelve Steps in my new way of living, giving, and forgiving. Today God does provide everything I have and everything I am. I was told one time that the ocean doesn't depend on the waves, but rather they are only part of the ocean. Reflecting about that helps me to revere the spiritual truth that God is in charge of my life; not my own self-will, doubts, stubbornness, fears, and insecurities. (My big storm waves...)

With total dedication to the Twelve-Step process, I am now aware that my soul responds to the slightest indication of belief from my conscious mind that a Divine Power is leading me to emotionally healthy ways of thinking and behaving. I use a small prayer, one of many I learned from the Scriptures as a child, and it always stayed with me: "God, I believe, but please help my unbelief." I used to keep searching for help with my doubts, and I used my own self-will and intelligence to try to answer any challenges. I'm aware today that my old self-will run riot is useless and I need to open myself up to receive love and wisdom from a Higher Power.

To be honest, occasionally I may not feel God's presence in a strong manner, usually because I've allowed too many mundane things to interfere with that connection. The truth is that He is always there for me. His light shines within me and His love nurtures me, whether I'm *aware of that or not.* When I feel lost, I can renew that consciousness of God by a spiritual reading, or from something in nature. I really don't need to tell Him anything; He is omnipotent and always knows what I'm thinking and feeling. I only need to close my eyes and silence my wayward mind in order to fully nurture my soul. The important thing is, I feel His presence in others. In that way, I am able to accept and respect them, just as they are in the moment—something I couldn't do until I went through a transformation with the Twelve Steps. I continually renew my Spirit through comfort given by others.

Believing in a Power much greater than myself is like a true friendship that cannot be threatened by anything else—except my lack of willingness, and I can see Him today as a never ending, trusted friend and confidant. I'm not the same person who entered the rooms of the program many twenty-four hours ago.

When taken twenty-four hours at a time, I have no fear of change. When I look at the people in the program who are walking the path ahead of me, I wish I were up there with them, but when I turn around and look at the people behind me, I realize, "I'm glad I'm not still back there." It all "works if we work it…"

# 19

## *Dreams and Goals*

Most of my goals and dreams were based on my expectations; consequently, I had to face many disappointments and heartbreak from ruined dreams. They were usually about the distant future and some day when, and the *hope* in the program seemed to also be about the future—so exactly where did that leave me? I discovered I needed to stay in the here and now and keep an open mind every moment of every day.

It's difficult to feel that a familiar door has closed, and occasionally that can leave me with a lot of emotional pain. I may not always understand why God closes some and opens certain others that allow me to have opportunities I never dreamed I could/would receive; but I keep my faith that He knows what He is doing, and He is definitely in charge.

First and foremost, I must seek the help of a Divine Power's will and guidance when planning dreams and goals for myself. Sometimes I wonder, how soon will my prayers be answered about a hoped for dream and goal? I have to stop and examine my actions to see if there could be something that's keeping me from reaching a definite goal. Usually what seems to be a slow response from Him is about my expectations of what He should/could be granting me—*my wishes!* But then, perhaps it's a matter of not paying attention to the messengers He is sending my way. Maybe I am so involved with what my desires are that I'm not looking at the particular door that He already has/or is opening for me. Almost daily I hear of, and experience, miracles in my great Twelve-Step program. God only wants what is best for me, and He is working on that, so I have to trust Him and just let it be for now.

It's necessary that I try to keep a happy balance in my emotional life, and when I set goals I make sure I can bridge the gap between motives and expectations. I need to determine if my motives and expectations are realistic. By doing that, I probably avoid setting myself up for failure.

I'm still attempting to heal the wounds from a few broken dreams because they are so painful to recall; however, the program teaches me that I do have to face any bad memories of days gone by and move on with my life. In other words, I have to believe that people are given "second chances." That's an old adage; however, I am convinced I'm proof of that and better late than never...

Before working the program, my dreams and goals were all part of the fantasy world I made up in the battle against the disease. Today, I can see that trying to live in a fantasy world is like being on a magic carpet ride to nowhere. Presently, I can look at my dreams and goals as challenges, no matter how old I may be. I can strive for them, and they are attainable by working the program. One day following another, I can take realistic steps to accomplish them. It takes an enormous amount of courage to attempt to reach some goals we may dream up, but it's written in the Scriptures, *"If God be for us, who can be against us?"*

With the help of a Higher Power, I can now accomplish almost anything that I make up my mind to do. If I keep thinking positively, I'll reach those goals—by deleting those negative tapes, those nasty little committees in my head that began in my childhood: "You'll never measure up" and "You're not good enough." I have to stop looking to others for my approval, and instead of thinking "I "won't" or I "can't," I need to change those thoughts into, *"I will."* The only approval I need is from my God, and He has made me aware now that when I accept that truth, I will succeed. The others in the race will have their own Power Greater to help them. I love the saying, "I own something," (my needs, feelings, etc.) because it's very reassuring. It convinces me that I am making progress.

When I do achieve a goal I have set for myself, I'm given many benefits. Some of these are self-confidence, self-respect, self-love, and whatever it was that I had to practice to get to that goal, I get to keep; hopefully forever.

When I took care of my precious granddaughter during the day for a few years, I watched her take her first wobbly steps and cheered and celebrated each one. However, years later, I neglected to cheer my own stumbling attempts to take the first few steps in my program—just another example of not concentrating on my own welfare. I have to remember that I am not in a race; I am simply learning to make progress with the Twelve Steps, and not trying to keep up with the people who are way ahead of me. My dreams and goals are all part of my journey, with no destination and a new way of looking at life, people, and circumstances.

Having dreams and goals means I am making choices today for my best welfare instead of allowing others to make those choices for me. The importance of that belief now is: I don't have to apologize to anyone for my doing that. I'm positive that my dreams and goals are all God's work. I'm in His hands, and I do not have to fear the resulting outcome.

Today, I am convinced that if I just put one foot in front of the other and handle whatever adjustments are necessary to achieve a goal, I'll eventually get there. Using the tools of the program now means I'm more likely to be successful in reaching them, through God and with God. One of my current main goals is to attempt to reach the highest awareness of spiritual understanding, at least as much as I possibly can, and in trying to reach that goal, I am slowly being healed.

I'm aware that there are no guarantees when I follow a special dream—just hope and confidence that my Power Greater is leading me out of my comfort zone to a better place. I'm so glad I had the courage to step out of the darkness of misery and self-pity and begin a new life when I did. I am surrounded now with positive-thinking people who understand my spirituality, and we support each other in our program beliefs.

# 20

## *Facing Reality*

For a long time I was in denial about the realities of living with alcoholism. I think I mentally escaped any problems by daydreaming that everything was going to be okay "some day"; if we could only do this or that, our lives would get better. But it never did get better, because that darn big pink elephant sat right in the middle of our home and wouldn't budge, no matter how hard I pushed! I detached by working as a secretary, having many hobbies: piano, advanced sewing, and other things, taking care of our precious daughters, and trying to be the "perfect" housewife. Everything had to be perfect in appearance, because I thought everyone else had a "perfect marriage." I know differently now.

Beginning with my childhood, I stuffed all of my feelings. I don't remember feelings ever being discussed by either parent. A lot of my behavior grew from living with a physically and verbally abusive mother; however, I can accept now that she was mentally unstable. She was part of a dysfunctional family as a child because of my grandfather's alcoholism and compulsive gambling.

I had a lot of imaginary friends as a child. I think I endured the lack of love and caring from my mother by doing that. Unfortunately, that pattern continued into my marriage. I thought some day I'd leave him and find someone who could love and care for me and be my best friend; then I would be happy. Living in a fantasy world only led me to live a lonely, isolated life except for others at my place of employment, although they never really knew me well either—only what I wanted them to know. With the help of others in my Twelve-Step Program, I came to believe that my happiness could only begin with me, and I had to keep the focus only on myself.

When I began working the Steps, I had no concept of who Mary-Glen might be. My way of trying to cope with a bad marriage was by not validating my feelings or verbally expressing them. Examining that in retrospect, I'm sure that was caused by fear of his bad temper and the fear of being pushed around at times. But God did keep me safe. There are words in a beautiful Psalm, *"Keep me as the apple of your eye."* I used those words a lot as comfort and a feeling of protection.

With the help of the principles in the Twelve Steps, I can now accept what and how I am feeling right at this moment. I internalized everything I possibly could in our Twelve Step literature; however, recovery didn't come by sharing what I learned in the literature. Rather, it came from what I discovered by *using the insights from it* when I had a similar situation in my own life to deal with. It all takes endless practice.

If I am to have meaningful relationships and discover my true self-worth, I must look for opportunities to enlighten others who are new to our program principles. I had a shadow world that I had built inside of me as a child as part of my way of escaping reality. I carried that world with me into a marriage that was being destroyed by the disease. My shadow world was full of the wishful thinking of "could have/should have" and "would have been." That type of escape, perhaps, was God's way of protecting me from an emotional breakdown, but at the time I didn't realize the harm it was doing to me. I wasn't aware that living in fantasy vs. reality was wasting my precious time on this earth.

Life is so very short, and I was not living it; I was only dreaming about living it. I was also destroying any chance I had of being happy in the here and now. Every time I wandered off into my perfect fantasy world, I developed more resentment, self-pity, and unhappy feelings about the way we lived.

Even worse, I couldn't see anything good about my actively drinking alcoholic husband, because I didn't see him as he really was. I compared him to the person I had dreamed up as my ideal companion in my shadow world, something I regret to say now that he could never measure up to. With enough time in the program, and with healing, I can see that he did have a lot of good qualities about him that I never allowed him credibility for.

It can sometimes still take me a while to accept the reality of what's flowing around me. Reality has some harsh stuff in it, and I don't always want to accept that this is the way it is. (Maybe, I still want to be in denial about some important events.) I want to make a lot of circumstances much nicer in my mind than they are in my real world. Therefore, today, I try to be completely objective about the situation, be aware, and accept that it is really happening to me. It is only by doing this process that I am able to make a choice not to let it become a priority that can affect my serenity.

I can do that today by focusing on my own issues in a situation with a lot of help from God. When I think about any situations in my past that made me react in a similar manner to the current challenge, I then examine whatever I perceive may have led me to believe I need to behave in that manner again. I look for any "payoff" I may not be aware I have benefited from in that self-destructive behavior. In this process, I am able to discover whether or not I am slipping back into old destructive behavior patterns and accept that this is the way I am—at least, for now.

I am free now to choose my attitude under any circumstances that flow my way—to choose my own way of living, with the help of my Higher Power. When I radiate spiritual compassion and love, I add value and meaning to my own life; and people are attracted to me. Coming from a lifetime of almost complete isolation with an active alcoholic, that is very meaningful to me.

Humility and honesty are of the utmost importance when I'm sharing my feelings with others, either one-to-one or in a group. Today I am positive that by telling my story and by my example of thinking and behaving, and others sharing theirs, we inspire newcomers to believe that the program will work for them. By each one sharing his/her own story and/or problem that he/she has found the solution to, by using the principles in each one of the steps, our Higher Power uses us to help each other. I, and others like me, am living proof that the Al-Anon Twelve Steps can lead us to a better way of living. It is indeed a Higher Power that restored me to sanity. I could never have arranged for that to happen by myself.

By this, I don't mean to say that reading my Al-Anon literature is not an important tool in working the program. The principles are very easy to understand, but also on occasion easy to forget. What does make the difference in my life is applying them on a daily basis to all that I do. I used to average about ten meetings per week in the first seven years or so. (I would be in three meetings two days per week.) It was not because I needed to socialize; I just needed to start feeling good about myself. I needed a sponsor who had a sponsor, who had walked this path before me. I needed to walk through the challenges that my Power Greater was giving me in order to find the gift in them of what I needed to learn and grow. Mainly because if I didn't learn from those challenges, He would send me more of the same until I did!

I am not perfect, and so I do not always apply these principles to all of my affairs. I am on a journey of "Progress not Perfection." (Another one of our Slogans.) My sponsor told me once—well, maybe more than once—that I would do what I needed to do when I'm ready to do it; and I was right where I needed to be, even if I'd rather have been somewhere else. When I discovered that I was acting in a way I didn't like, I needed to get back to work on me. Sometimes I 'd find myself in a pretty dark place before I was ready to climb out of that hole again. I have seen now what this program and a Power Greater has accomplished in others lives, and I am now experiencing the true joy of my new way of living.

Today I go to my meetings as a newcomer would: hoping to have an open trusting mind and trying to hear the message my Higher Power wants me to hear. Listening to newcomers reminds me that I'm not much different than they are, and listening to long-timers reminds me that I have a lot more growing to do. By coming back every week and reading our literature every day, I can keep my emotions, my head, my responses, and my reactions balanced and know I am in the process of recovery.

When I first came to Al-Anon, I was trying to control, but did not accept tough situations and people for what they were: emotionally sick. I was magnetically attracted to needy people at that time; they seemed to be waiting for me to come along before they jumped and attached themselves to me with their emotional hook. My sponsor asked me to write out some of my story, and I was amazed to recall for her all of the horrible things that had happened to me. As I wrote, I thought, "Look at me. I survived all of this. Wow, what a saint and martyr I am!"

Today, I know that my story is not unique. In fact, I am probably just average. I've had an easier life than some, but a much more difficult life than others; however, I do believe now that I myself am one of the program miracles. I had a victory over living with the disease because I'm recovering now. And today, I don't have to reenact any part of my story when confronted with similar circumstances.

I didn't know what "unmanageable" meant in the First Step when I began working Step One. I decided later, in working the program, that it had been obvious that my life was unmanageable; I had already admitted that fact. Actually, I had lived it for forty years; however, I didn't have what it took to manage my own life.

Facing reality now means that I live life on life's terms. A long-time member shared with me that; the Second Step uses the word "could" restore me to sanity, which indicates that restoration to sanity is not automatic. Admitting honestly that I was powerless relieved me of a sense of shame and blame against myself for feeling guilty of abandoning him. The truth is that he had abandoned me many years before, when he continued to progressively consume more and more alcohol. After all, as we say in the program, "Only an insane person would continue to do day to day what he/she knows is impossible."

Other members taught me that I am the only one responsible for my dreams, goals, and feelings. I had to change my perspectives from my old way of living before the program in order to do that. I always had looked to my parents as a child, then my actively drinking alcoholic husband for my happiness, and that only gave them power over me. I had no choice as a child but to look to my parents, but as an adult, eventually I *should* have learned to value my own opinions, respect my own intelligence, and value my own worth.

Today I ask my Higher Power on a daily basis to help me remember to respect myself enough to listen to my real feelings. The feelings I didn't recognize and couldn't *name, understand, or own,* before working the Steps. Those feelings had been in my soul all of my life and just festered until they were like a poison destroying me. Working the program helps me "Feel, deal, and heal them."

My exaggerated perceptions used to have the power to interfere with the peace and harmony I longed for in all the moments I was blessed with. They still can do that if I try to build a fortress of resentment out of a few small grains of misunderstanding.

Most of my life, I'd obsessed about him, the active alcoholic, what he was doing or not doing! *He was the one* making my life miserable, and I let him know that every chance I got. When I came to the Twelve-Step rooms, they weren't talking about what they were doing to help an alcoholic; they were talking about what they were doing to help themselves. Gradually, it began to sink in, and I began to focus on what I could do for myself. One advantage of this new way of thinking was that: I finally discovered what my own interests and talents were. I began taking time to do what I needed to do for myself; and most importantly of all, to make the things I wanted to do a priority in my life. Selfish? Perhaps a little, but today I see that as not being self-"less" and that is definite progress for me.

Some experts state that you can learn into your nineties, the same way a five-year old does—it just takes longer, and time is going faster for me every year! I have to decide what my own life really means to me. Do I have an "I'm too old" attitude, or do I seek out new things to learn? I am responsible for the quality of my life and how I live it. I am also learning never to let one door close without looking for the new one God has opened; to look for new challenges and keep working on self-discovery, regardless of how old I am. I find that today I am so busy enjoying my new self; I don't have time to notice that I am getting older!

If I had never worked the Steps, I am positive that the greatest regret I could ever have known would have been to live this life and never know who I really am—who I was meant to be—the uniquely special person that only lives in my body. With your help, I'm discovering the true personality God intended me to become; and most importantly, I really love her. Self-love helps me reach out to others instead of living in isolation as I did in my former marriage. There's a program saying I love: "How can you be in a great relationship with God, or anyone else, if you're not in a great relationship with yourself?" I know I've accomplished that now, thanks to my great fellowship named Al-Anon.

The Twelve Steps continue helping me to take the gifts that I have been given and use them in many wonderful ways. They are also helping me make a better gift of myself to God by becoming a healthier and more positive person. The more I can accept and love my humanness, the better I am able to do the same for others in my life. I believe our Twelve-steps program is another gift from God, for which I am very grateful.

# 21

## *Gratitude*

*"Let all that I am today be in service to Thy will, Lord…"* Mary-
Glen Scot

Every act that I do for my Higher Power must be with gratitude, kindness, and love for all. Giving of myself in service work in Al-Anon is the highest tribute I can pay to all others who have served before me, and who serve with me now. I give whatever I've been given—all that I can possibly offer, for it makes me feel worthwhile; something I never felt before working the Twelve Steps. Feeling gratitude is an important prescription for troubled minds in our fellowship.

The first Thanksgiving I was an Al-Anon member, I went to bed feeling very sad and harboring lots of self-pity because I was divorced and living alone. I pictured every face of a program friend who had offered me unconditional love and hope for a new life, and one by one told God "thank you" for that person. As a result, I was able to fall asleep in a much better frame of mind.

One of the many things I accomplished early on in the program was to have an "attitude of gratitude," and I did that with the help of others who taught me I have a choice as to whether I am grateful or not. Over the years, choosing to be grateful has made my life go more smoothly. It is the fastest path to peace and serenity. I was caught in an atmosphere of negativity growing up, and I've had to combat it ever since, so I need to rely on something to pull me out of sadness. Gratitude is a fast remedy for that.

Sometimes I become stranded on the "pity poor me" throne, usually because I'm unhappy with my body because I have scoliosis that was untreated when I was a child. That's when God puts someone right in front of my eyes who is afflicted with a much more severe physical condition than I have. For example, maybe I just happen to drive by the young man in our neighborhood who rides in a wheeled contraption because he has no legs—then I get off my "poor me" in a hurry. I'm able to have gratitude for all of the blessings I have been given.

One day, going into church, I saw a little girl being unloaded in a wheel chair from a van and it looked as if her limbs were withering away. How fortunate it made me feel about my own physical problem when I saw her that day. I thought, "Maybe I didn't have the love and kindness I needed from my mother as a child, but I was able to grow up and have arms and legs that are basically healthy, to get married, and have two truly wonderful daughters. That sweet little girl looks as if she will probably not grow to be an adult, get married, and have children as I did." It made my cup overflow with gratitude for all of God's blessings in my world today. That was the awareness and gift in the lesson He wanted me to have that particular Sunday morning.

Each day I mentally, or in writing, do a gratitude list of five things I am thankful for. My sponsor told me "five one liners and no more," because its difficult for me to be succinct. This exercise has helped shift my focus from the negative to the positive, and when I slip into old negative thinking ways, such as self-pity, I don't have to stay there long. I have become a more thoughtful, courteous person by making sure I give special thanks to the people who help me and bless my life; from people who serve me in a store to my beloved sweetheart in my life now, and my family.

I have no tangible evidence to show a reason why I have never been financially broke, but I'm positive it's due to the Grace of God. I now have complete serenity and contentment, and gratitude for all I've been blessed to receive from Him. As we say in our fellowship, "He can do for me what I cannot do for myself," and that is one of my greatest gifts of Al-Anon.

A Twelve Step mentor once told me that during any suffering in my life, I should look for the "gift" in the experience. She explained that God had allowed the lesson to come into my life for a reason and for my ultimate good. And I could expedite the process, if I could accept the situation, find the gift, and thank Him for it.

Today, I carry that perspective further: I look to see what the lesson can be in a challenge, and then if I can't handle the "trial" (the problem) I do whatever footwork I'm capable of doing. I am then able to surrender the rest to my Power Greater Than Myself, and He grants me peace once again.

# 22

## *Judgment of Others*

By using self-honesty, I can see that previously I tended to use the flaw of being judgmental to see myself as *better than* or *holier than thou.* I couldn't have tolerance, understanding, kindness, or love for all others until I stopped judging my own self so harshly. Even today, I hear a committee in my head occasionally that's at war with my true inner being.

I have to remember that: I don't know what another human being's emotional experiences were in the past, just as they probably aren't knowledgeable of mine. I see (judge) them most of the time simply based on very little knowledge of their true self.

This awareness was really brought home to me these past few years in the Al-Anon groups. There were two harshly critical people I couldn't stand to be around when I first began the program. I thought they were toxic to me, and I preferred not to be in the same meeting with them. Strange, today I love both of those people "in a very special way," as we say in our fellowship; however, they have changed very little. It is my perception of them that has changed. Yes, they do have caustic tongues at times and my concern is that they may unmindfully hurt a newcomer's feelings, but they do have a lot of good qualities that I failed to acknowledge when I first knew them. I am aware now that I should not judge others, but simply accept them as they are.

My program sponsor taught me to ask myself, "Do I need to find a flaw in someone else and tear him or her down in order to build myself up?" In our program, when we judge someone else's behavior, we're taught that it's usually because we have similar traits ourselves; this is known as "Spot It, You Got It!" I must try to remember that I'm not their judge and jury." Only their Higher

Power owns that status. Recovery means changing whatever needs to be changed, and that's why a lot of us are in the Twelve-Step program. I heard someone share recently, "We're so good at seeing someone else's mistakes—too bad we can't just trade places with them."

We have a slogan, "Live and Let Live," that I try to keep in mind in relationships with others. It's almost impossible to make progress in the program if I continue to be hurt, offended, or consumed by the behavior and attitudes of other people. I have to accept, and surrender to God, the knowledge that every person He created on this earth does have the right to live as he/she chooses, freed from my perspectives, criticism, judgment, contempt, and resentments. If what they are doing is immoral or illegal, then they have to suffer the consequences. If someone is doing something unacceptable to me, I can discuss this with them and set boundaries if I have to. If they feel they owe me any amends, I have a choice to accept, forgive them, and move on; or remove myself from the friendship.

An old adage that really helps me is: "When I can put myself in the other person's place, I am less likely to put him in his place." Now when I find myself judging someone in my mind, I tell myself "stop" and immediately look for something that is good in that person instead of mentally criticizing what they are saying or doing.

# 23

## *Keep the Focus on Me*

My Higher Power gifts my Spirit today with much love, generosity, patience, tolerance, joy and peace. All of these things represent more wealth than any material things I have ever accumulated, and I can share this wealth of my Spirit with others now. The more I share with them, the more will be multiplied in our worldwide fellowship. I've learned, with the help of Al-Anon, that my Higher Power has first priority, and after that I keep the focus on me.

I used to be an expert at meddling in others' relationships, particularly my in-laws. I was almost positive in my marriage to an actively drinking alcoholic that if we would just move far away from the others in his family, and my parents, why we would have a lot less problems. That thinking was just another example of justification and qualification for our dilemmas. My goodness, it couldn't be his drinking, or my crazy reactions—could it?

We were always subjected to the usual family get-together type of thing in my first marriage. Most of them were Irish or Scottish, and we had the usual "rows" (their word for arguments) every time alcoholic beverages were served.

When there was a problem between two of my in-laws, I always had to get involved and fix it all up for them. I just couldn't have disputes or hullabaloos around me, not if I could help it. They looked at me as if I was their sweet, patient, loving little angel in the family that never yelled at anyone, or got offended or angry, and that stayed as my role for many years.

I used to try to interpret what each one of them said, and then I'd think of an explanation of what I thought that meant. From there, I'd tell first one, then the other, what he/she said and what I felt he/she really meant to say when they said what they did, and I'd try to smooth things over between them. That didn't work; the war between them would get worse, and I'd still be in the middle. Then the strangest thing would happen; they'd have a horrendous battle, settle their differences, and end up the best of friends. Maybe it was because I got out of the way; but I'd be left on the outside because of my interference.

The sad thing is, I never was able to understand it all. Why I was left out of his/her newly established, understanding relationship with each other? Then I found my Twelve-Step groups and learned about "Mind Your Own Business." That was an interesting development in my life, to say the least. My goodness, couldn't they see that I was only being "helpful"?

Keeping the focus on myself was impossible before working the program. The antics of the alcoholic were so much more immediate and dramatic than anything I was doing, and since I was the only sober one, I had to fix things as best as I could. The alcoholic loved my role, because I did my part in getting things done, and his! And he could find fault with me for whatever I did, no matter how well I handled it. Those characteristics in our relationship did start to have a drastic effect on my life, and I developed a rather poor self-image because I really wasn't fixing anything at all, nor was I getting any positive results. I was also becoming very angry because obviously he didn't give a d— about my wants or needs. But I should have been questioning myself, why should anyone pay attention to something I was ignoring myself?

With the help of others who were sharing solutions in meetings, I gradually learned to change my way of thinking about him and began to focus more on what *I could do for myself.* There were still many crises with him, but my help became more constructive and less controlling on his behalf.

Part of my soul is still restless and continually searching for something, it knows not what; only a Power Greater Than Myself can satisfy that need, that longing. All others in the program are helping me in that process.

# 24

# *Learning to Live in the Here and Now*

*"Therefore do not be anxious for tomorrow, for tomorrow will take care of itself. Each day has enough troubles of its own." Matthew 6:34*

As a young adult, I thought those who used the philosophy, "Live for today, for tomorrow we die" were irresponsible, and used it only as a pretext and a cop-out, just another excuse to spend money foolishly. To live it up and go into debt more than they could ever possibly pay back in their lifetime. Nowadays, I view all of that through a changed perspective. I think of living in today in a positive light now, more in a spiritually and emotionally secure way, because I now believe that God wants me to feel happy, content, and free to live life to its fullest, one day at a time.

When my mind was full of regrets over the past and full of anxieties about my future, I became too overwhelmed to cope with my here and now. Some experiences still cause me to have expectations about the future; trying in vain to stay one step ahead of where I am in the moment. When I find that I'm doing that, I'm aware that I am not living in today.

My world is filled with simple moment-to-moment pleasures now, and I am blessed and filled with joy when I take the time to notice and appreciate them. Sometimes, things beyond my control affect my ability to notice these pleasures, these gifts. If I do a fast inventory, I usually discover that I need to return my thoughts to the present moment. "Stay in the moment and speak in the moment"—I must have heard that dozens of times from my service sponsor before I finally figured out how to get there.

It seems to me that from the time we are born, someone should teach us that we have only these twenty-four hours to live, and maybe we'd make an effort to try to live life to the maximum, every moment of each day. After all, we truly only have a numbered amount of tomorrows on this earth anyway. I struggled with staying in the moment before the program. I used to live for the "when" and the "ifs," but those things never happened, for the reason that they were all based on my assumptions and/or expectations.

I was so used to living in the past, the future, and a place I now call "never-never land," where I escaped in my mind when today and the future were too horrible to think about. The current moments were never a satisfactory place to be because I lived in fantasy and kept the door tightly closed on any actual reality I faced. With the help of other members in Al-Anon, I began to realize and accept that I could not go back and change the past, or step forward into the future. God gives me this gift of today only twenty-four hours at a time and I use it to the best of my abilities and talents.

I do have to consider my future: Make sure I have insurance needs, a legal will to protect my loved ones, make reservations for flights and hotel rooms for a planned vacation, and so forth. All of these things are under my control and are part of what we call in our program, "Doing the footwork," but the rest is up to my Higher Power.

I couldn't keep letting past scenes of bitterness and regrets ruin my life one day following another. I'm still not certain if all of my love for my former husband had been completely destroyed when the end of our marriage occurred, or if some still lingered. I know he was extremely sad when he realized I was finally going to leave him. I still have sad visual scenes in my mind that can surface of those last few days with him, and they can be painful now and then. If my Al-Anon family hadn't been there for me, I may have, *even one more time,* returned to live with him. And that would have been only to fill *his need* to have me, because of my feelings of guilt and sorrow for him.

Due to the way I shared in meetings, even a year or so later my sponsor and a few close program friends were still concerned I'd do that. Those memories of past unhappiness had to be dealt with. I couldn't let those "what if" and "if only" videos keep replaying—recirculating—in my mind. I had to forgive the way we were. Today, I can quickly hit the delete button on those old videos in my mind when they pop up, and I have peace with the past. I can live in the present precious moments. I like the old saying: "Today is a gift that's why we call it the present." If I keep busy setting goals for the future, I might forget to live in the present, and *that* is exactly what I did before finding our great fellowship.

In the past, a feeling of hopelessness and despondency would cause a committee in my head to want to plan every possible scenario and solve every possible combination of problems *before they would even happen!* I'd start to exaggerate everything, and pretty soon I'd be controlled completely by my own fear and confusion about the unknown. Gradually, with the help of God and the program, I'm beginning to release my negative thinking, and have gratitude for all of the great things God does for me, moment to moment.

When I find myself leaving the present moments, I remind myself now that the future is not today's problem. Most of my life, I lived in an unhealthy home situation and relationship, which affected my ability to find solutions that would lead me to peace and harmony. I joined the Twelve-Step groups and let others influence my thinking. (I'd been doing that for years, anyway, but it was influenced by others' negative attitudes.) I listened and reasoned things out in my chosen Al-Anon Family and slowly began to change for the better. I now realize I cannot postpone any unplanned challenges until I have all of the solutions I think I need. I have to step out in faith, take risks, and do the best footwork I can to meet my needs in my here and now, with God's help.

In the past I'd use emotional runaways when life circumstances overwhelmed me, but now, when I start feeling hopeless and helpless, I pray, "Help me to stay in the moment, God." Others in Al-Anon constantly remind me: "Even grief, terror, or extreme pain is manageable—one second at a time!"

I now understand that there is a difference between going back into the past in an attempt to blame someone/something for our misery, versus going back there to try to heal, to forgive, and to forget. I journeyed back in time to examine the perceptions I internalized as a child; those things that cause some reactions in me as an adult. I didn't want to write about some of those painful memories; however, my sponsor encouraged me to write about my experiences as far back as I could remember, and I did. I found that I had painful videos stored in my mind that began as young as two years old. (My mother was astonished when I talked about them; she probably hoped I wouldn't remember the incidences.) Later, my sponsor told me: If you truly want to know yourself, write your life story.

As I wrote my life story, and examined my sad childhood experiences from memories locked within, I realized I had suffered wounds: Emotionally, physically, socially, and spiritually. And I'm sure now that, at one point in time I must have felt that I wasn't worthy of love from God, or from anyone else. Slowly, I began to change my former feelings about myself, and I began to have enough self-confidence to set goals for my own future. I discovered that I could feel the feelings I couldn't name in the past, couldn't describe, and didn't even know existed in my inner being.

Before working the Steps, I'd get so wrapped up in future plans that I missed out on a lot of great moments in my today, and I'd obsess about things I could do nothing about at all. I am now able to make choices that are very self-empowering, and not let my inner child (who can still be fearful at times) make those decisions for me. When watching TV, I can pick up the remote and change the channel, and it's possible to do that with my stinking thinking or whatever I'm obsessing about at the moment. I can change the channel in my mind to whatever/wherever I wish it to be.

When I'm confident that I am in God's care, I can accept whatever life is sending me because I'm assured it's all in His hands. Consciously choosing to live in the present moment provides me with peace and comfort. The future hasn't arrived yet and no amount of planning about what I'll do tomorrow is going to guarantee that's what is going to happen. For the present is in today only. That thought alone helps me keep my serenity, and my sanity

I try not to deny myself happy thoughts about the joy I anticipate we'll have in future activities; however, I won't let any unrealistic expectations build up and cause me to have a bitter, emotional letdown if things change and don't go the way we had planned. That would only, temporarily at least, destroy my serenity. I cannot rewrite God's script for my life; I can only make rough drafts of what I'd like to see happen in the future.

My living moments had become so cluttered with regrets and worries that I had difficulty handling the "now." I am sure I missed a lot of wonderful experiences in my life that way, but I've learned to make peace with my past. With the help of my Twelve-Step family, I can learn from my mistakes and hopefully not repeat them; at least not too often. If I must, I can work through any dark, painful memories now and come out with a sense of peace and healing. In the past, I practiced self-will-run-riot and I ended up doing things, being in places and relationships, that I had kept begging my God for, but felt I did not receive answers to my "pleas." So I took the actions and thinking I needed to do to have my Mary-my-way-be-done, without waiting for His guidance and wisdom. That proved to be a disastrous way of life for me.

My lesson from all of that is: Life is much too short to be weighed down with problems that are not mine to own and that I am unable to resolve. No amount of obsessing can change what has gone before either; however, I can give it all to my God and let it be. I can let go of my fears about tomorrow and next week and trust that He is already there. I now believe that today is all I can manage, and He gives me choices about how I approach each new day. I can choose to remain in the present and enjoy what today brings, rather than allow worry and regrets of the past to linger in my mind. Of course, there are days when this is not easy to do, but I can ask my Higher Power for help. He can guide me back to the wonder and serenity I desire; if I live in the moment.

Old reactions can still sometimes makes me look to tomorrow, hoping for a better day when I expect everything to be wonderful, instead of being here right now and working with what I've got. But the Serenity Prayer reminds me, if I keep looking to tomorrow I'll never get the peace I need in my life

Today, I do the footwork to the best of my ability and leave the rest up to my God. I'm confident now, things will turn out the way they're meant to be, but only in His time. My daily goal now is to simply live in peace and harmony with others. At day's end, I'll feel rewarded by doing that, because I will have accomplished what the Son of God hoped for—"Love one another."

# 25

## *Our Children*

I will not be sharing about our two precious daughters, or my one darling granddaughter in this book. I have a wonderful, loving, caring relationship with them and am very proud of them. They both got married very young and were later divorced; however, they have both been happily married for many years, are emotionally healthy, and both have executive positions and earn good salaries. They, or my granddaughter or son-in-laws, have never had the desire to take drugs or drink—and I thank my God on a regular basis on bended knees for that blessing. After my divorce, my older daughter told me one evening when we were having a discussion, "Oh Mother, I used to pray that you'd leave him when I was in high school." I cried when she told me that, because I thought I was doing the best thing for them at the time by helping them continue to live in a nice home. Subsequently, it occurred to me while working the Steps that I should have consulted them about *what we* wanted to do about their father's drinking and abuse. I should have given them the privilege of being involved in any decisions I made about our common welfare. (Those were some more of my "should have's…")

There were some challenges that came up that we were able to resolve, due to being a dysfunctional family because of someone's alcoholism; however, I have no intention or purpose to share those in public. I have heard speakers in our program share about their children's problems; nevertheless, it's my humble opinion that I would be seriously breaking not only my daughters' anonymity, but also possibly damaging their personal lives, if I were to speak about those problems in a meeting; or in my writing. I feel that is theirs to handle. My world is only in the here and now, and our daughters' personal lives are theirs to own.

When I decided to separate from their father, my daughters were concerned for my safety and security, and my older daughter asked me if I'd like to move back home to where we'd lived for over forty years. She suggested that she get a larger home with possibly a guesthouse or separate in-law quarters, and I agreed that would probably be the best thing for me to do. They did find a beautiful home that was suitable for all of us, and I saw it with them, and they made an offer of the full price on it.

The neighborhood was very beautiful and I have always loved the climate where the girls grew up; regardless, I was having serious doubts about living with them. I am very independent and I had fears that I would interfere with their lives by trying to get them to do things "Mary-my-way." My mind was so confused and I cried a lot the few days I was looking at real estate with them. I thought maybe I should buy a small townhouse in the city we had moved to, except I just didn't know what to do at all. Well, God decided for me.

A few days after I returned to the house I still shared with my ex-husband, I got a call from my family and they said that the owner at the last minute could not sell the home she had lived in most of her life, and raised her family in. I commiserated with her, and empathized (even though I was almost thirty years younger), because she had developed the most beautiful English garden—all in full spring blossom—I'd ever seen in the average middle-income home. Being an avid gardener all of my life, I would have loved to have it. She was almost ninety, and her son was very upset with her because he felt she should be in an assisted living home, but she had a clear mind and decided not to sell her home, so our plans to buy that house were denied. In retrospect, I feel that once again God was following His plan for my life and everything was going in the proper *Divine direction*.

I loved an older development of town homes in the city I now live, which had lots of grass and large pine trees, and the streets were all *Scottish names!* A few weeks later a small one went up for sale, and I knew my destiny was being fulfilled. I am still living in that development with my second husband. We are extremely happy with our home, and I feel that God arranged it all.

When I decided to stay in this city, which is about three-hundred-miles from where my daughters live, I didn't realize how that would affect my granddaughter. I had spent a lot of time with her as she was growing up, and we had really bonded in a special way. I was so wrapped up in my own self-pity and confusion that I hadn't thought of how *she would feel* about me being so far away. She did feel sadness, but she resolved that by deciding she could fly every so often by herself to see her grandma, or come with her parents. I am extremely blessed to have a loving, caring family.

I don't see my loved ones as often as we'd all like to. We all live extremely busy lives. Nevertheless, I know they love me very much and are happy for me that I now live in harmony, true inner peace, and contentment, and have a wonderful companion to share that with.

# 26

## *People Pleasing Behavior*

When I was a newcomer, my desire to do service work was based on my own need for approval from others; we call that people pleasing behavior in Al-Anon. I always looked to them to make me feel better and validate my feelings. Due to a lack of confidence in my abilities and talents, I was very motivated by what others thought of me, and I was emotionally sick from living with alcoholism. I really believed that I was only using acceptable actions and behavior if I were hearing from other people that I was helpful, wonderful, and exceptionally generous. Deep within my spirit I felt that I was definitely not okay; but as long as I kept smiling and being helpful, I thought I'd win the approval and love from others I longed for.

Most of my life before working the Steps, I compared myself to others, and as a result of low self-esteem, on a scale of 1-10, I'd end up putting myself at the very bottom. As a child, I looked to others for approval because of unmet needs for love from an emotionally sick mother. From the time I was very young, I kept trying to please her by doing housework or cooking because I thought I would "earn" her love that way. I did the same thing in my first marriage. I humbled myself and became humiliated in return by both my mother and husband. How could I possibly be true to my own "self" when I had practiced so much care giving of others?

Any signs of disapproval or rejection from someone made me depressed. When I began to feel like a truly worthwhile person, with the help of my sponsor and program friends, I became less concerned with what others thought, about anything, actually! Other Al-Anons (and AA members) help me with their insights and accomplishments; however, one of the greatest joys in my life today is being true to my own inner being and values. I am free now to be my own genuine, unique self.

My sponsor asked me to write about the following two questions: Do I need to have people act in a certain way in order for me to be happy? Do I want them to behave in a special way toward me? Writing about those led me to believe that I needed to speak up and let people know how I feel about certain interactions. As a recovering people pleaser, I have to accept that not everyone will like what I have to say and that life is not a popularity contest.

The voices of the old committees in my head can still pop up and drive me crazy at times with the things that they tell me "I can't do" or "shouldn't do." Those little committees are usually the voices from the past that torment me when I have not been using our acronyms, "HALT" (Don't let yourself get too Hungry, Angry, Lonely, or Tired) and "THINK" (Is this comment from me Thoughtful, Honest, Intelligent, Necessary, or Kind?) They even can threaten me with failure if I am taking the risk of trying to accomplish something new. I was taught to tell them to "get lost," or that "their input is not needed at this time." Those unacceptable voices are gradually becoming dimmer with more time working the Twelve Steps and more trust in my Higher Power, and my own abilities.

I no longer blame or have self-pity about my childhood or my marriage. I can honor my dignity and self-respect. I can love and accept myself as I am, and I'm learning that I should not look to others to evaluate my self-worth; who the authentic Mary-Glen is. When I would people please, I made myself feel like a victim or a martyr. I like the saying from our other program, "Get off the cross; we need the wood." I try to remember on a daily basis that I have *choices about my attitudes.*

I can think of my good qualities and look at my self-worth now as being able to love other people unconditionally; by saying a kind word, giving a sincere compliment, writing a considerate note, or just taking time out from a busy day to appreciate another human being. I remind myself to look for good qualities like those when I do my daily Tenth Step inventory; it helps my self-confidence and lets me see my progress, not perfection.

My Higher Power gives me the power to feel good about myself now, regardless of my achievements, and whether or not other people validate those feelings. I will forever be a work in progress, and I try to truly believe that change is now my friend, and not my enemy. That's not to say that change won't sometimes be scary and upsetting to me, but it is a lot less frightening when I remember that I do have power over myself, with His help. I've never found a magic power "button" in the program that can be pushed and I am changed or "magic slippers to click"; only God holds that Power, but I'm aware now that positive attitudes get positive results. Others can notice the change in me before I do, and they have. I had to learn to love and respect myself before others could truly love and respect me in return. When I tend to my own spiritual needs, I make it possible for others to see that special light in me that they may just want to participate in.

I used to be the world's best caregiver of everyone else. Today, I look at care giving as a gift, if I use it wisely, and I can find a happy balance to use in nurturing others and myself. Life is constantly changing, and so am I. When I can treat myself with self-love and approval, then I know I'm recovering. Part of learning to love myself and not people please is that I concentrate only on my own inventory, not that of others. (Not judging or condemning anyone.)

I am learning that I am not responsible for other people's actions, so I don't have to feel guilty and useless when they do not behave according to Mary-my-way's plan. I allow others the dignity of choosing to behave, as they will, whether or not I like what I see in them. They are doing what I also do best: simply being themselves. I have the power to feel good about myself, regardless of my achievements, even if others do not validate my efforts.

My unhappy feelings of the past no longer have power over me. I've done lots of work on my inner child, and today when I feel sad or down, I think of the beautiful child that is within me. I tell her, "We're going to be okay." Then I feel God's love flowing through me, and once again I have His peace within me. Through His grace, I feel I am one of our program's walking miracles, and I regularly remind myself how far I have come with His help.

I used to keep compromising myself for everyone else. I still have to be aware if I start asking myself, "What will people think if I do this? Will they think I'm strange, I'm mean, or what will they think of me?" Today it doesn't matter, because I think I'm great; thanks to my loving Twelve-Step family. The approval of others is enjoyable and I can accept compliments now without denying them, but my serenity is not dependent upon them. One of the advantages of having a good, strong connection with a Power Greater Than Myself is that my focus became, "What will He think if I do this? What will He think about me?" which is all that really matters. When I have my God to look up to for standards and what He expects of me, then it makes no difference in the world what others think of or expect of me.

# 27

## *Reactions, and Changing My Behavior*

The biggest problem is usually my reaction to the problem. I used to live as if I thought I had power to manage not only my own life, but also the lives of all those around me. For years, that false illusion deceived and almost destroyed me.

Every so often, I feel overwhelmed emotionally by incidents and circumstances that life is offering me, and I want to do a physical or emotional runaway, as I did before the program; however, I know today that I can examine where those feelings *are coming from.* Now and then they turn out to be reactions to something in my past; consequently, I work on finding solutions to combat them. But there are challenges that I just have to admit I can't do anything about, so I put them in my God Box (my lovely things for God to do box).

Ah—my feelings! I find that each time I am in a new experience that reminds me of an old experience, the old buttons are pushed and I once again act as I did in the past. I respond by reacting, and my reactions often are not valid or related to what is happening at the moment. The past is stored in my subconscious mind, and in a similar situation my subconscious responds and my conscious mind is fooled into thinking that the past is now!

For example, one time Paul accused me (jokingly) of putting something away that he needed and couldn't find. Later he found it in his desk and said, "Oh, I'm sorry, sweetie." I said that was okay, but then for some reason I went into a big "funk" of sadness in my mind. All he had said was "I'm sorry"; consequently, I had to sit down and think about why his remark made me feel sad. After meditating about my dilemma, I decided it was because my former husband always said—sometimes umpteen times a day—"I'm sorry." But he only *said* those words; he never changed his behavior to compensate for his "sorry," so I was reacting to the words, "I'm sorry." (I notice now that Paul will say, "I apologize." Smile.)

In the beginning, I was taught that while it may be true that another's behavior could affect me, it doesn't necessarily mean it has the power to take over my thinking and my actions. I used to justify my irrational behavior as being a result of theirs. I kept on doing that until I learned that I did not have to take offense just because it was offered to me. If another person picked up a rope and invited me into a tug-a-war, I could simply leave the rope lying, walk away, and not react. What a concept. *Besides which, no one can push a rope!*

Today I use sayings and slogans such as, "Don't just do something—sit there!" or "How important is it?" Sure, I can still react, but I try to save my lightning-quick reactions for those times when it's beneficial to do so—as when a life is in danger—or the last parking place close to the meeting is about to be taken by someone else. (Just joking!)

I have discovered that I am the slave of the person who gets me to react to their behavior, especially when that person fully intended for me to react the way I did. (I am giving them power over my actions and behavior.) Of course, there are exceptions to this principle; for example, when someone tells a very funny joke and I react with laughter. My point of view today is that I can make a conscious decision whether or not I want to react. Is it really okay for me to react, or am I falling into a carefully planned trap? (My first actively drinking alcoholic husband had a monopoly on that one.) I can make the proper response that's right for me by carefully examining each situation. There's a big difference between *when I am reacting, and when I'm merely responding.* When I'm reacting, I'm out of control. When I am responding calmly, I'm not, because a Divine Power is guiding my thoughts.

Once in a while I try to guess at what another person's motives appear to be in a situation. I stop and ask myself, "What did I say or do that made them take that action?" or "Why did I react to it the way I did?" At other times I ask myself: "Does what happened in the moment make an important difference to me?" or "Am I merely making a big deal out of some insignificant words or behavior on the part of the other person?"

Often it's simply a matter of asking myself, "Is the other person offering an opinion I didn't ask for?" They are certainly entitled to their opinions, as I am mine. Occasionally, I have to think, "Is the behavior of the other person really directed at me?" After working the program for many years, I decided that not everything is about me. I can now look dispassionately at the behavior of others, and often discover that it had nothing whatever to do with me. I just happened to be in the same space and time when they decided to act that way. It is not my problem—*unless I decide to make it mine by reacting.*

Another difference for me between reacting and responding is this: I don't "think" when I react, but I do "think" before I respond. Using the slogans and knowing I have *choices* gives me the basic tools with which to decide when I want to react and when I don't. However, if I slip and react, I don't "beat up" on myself today, but resolve to continue seeking progress in this area.

When I keep working on making changes in myself, I find that where I used to react with hurt feelings and anger, I now act with love and compassion. I am no longer a victim of life; I am a survivor with choices. In all I do, I strive for progress; accept that I have done my best. When I react, I give my power away; when I politely respond, I don't. It is not easy at times, but it works. I use the Twelve Steps as tools for living in peace and my own comfort.

# 28

## *Resentments and Anger Can Slowly Destroy Us*

The words I let come out of my mouth and tongue can create love, trust, peace and harmony both for me and for my loved ones; or they can create an atmosphere of living hell. Today, I try to be careful in my choice of words. In the beginning of our relationship, Paul taught me, "We can agree to disagree."

I accepted unacceptable behavior in my first marriage, and my life did become a living hell. A percentage of that was caused by my actions and reactions. I was slow to anger, but when I did, I used it like an "explosive weapon" against the person who had caused my pain. I guess it made me feel that I was the one in control; that I was the one with the power in the situation. I've surrendered that type of behavior, and I am aware today that only God has the controlling power over someone else's actions.

Resentment is only a feeling. I can wallow in it, or I can listen to what my body is trying to tell me when I feel that way, then I can decide what, if anything, needs to be done about the situation. It was with the help of others in the program that I learned to pay attention and think about why I was resentful and what I could do about it. I'm still learning how to do this, but today, when I realize I'm resentful, I try my best to look at my part in the situation. Occasionally, it's difficult to determine my part, and other times I don't want to see the truth, but I always feel much better when I face up to my part and what I can do. I also need to forgive others and myself.

In the past, I would do just about anything to have peace and harmony. As a result, I would repress a lot of my feelings; stuff them inside so they wouldn't be noticed. They would stay there and ferment until something major would occur and I'd then have the excuse I needed to explode. Or I'd use the silent treatment a lot. Silence is a blessing in some instances, but not if I am using it to show someone that I can't tolerate their behavior.

We have three "Ws" in the program.

1.  Whose problem is it?

2.  What is my part in it?

3.  Where does the action begin?

After mentally asking myself these questions and accepting that I have done all of the footwork to the best of my ability, usually the action is to "Let it Go" and let God take over the situation. He does that much better than I do, anyway. As we say in the program, "I have to remember: I would not have to forgive someone if I had not first judged and condemned him/her."

I learned that anger is just a feeling, an emotion and not a shortcoming; and that's okay. I can't help having the anger, the feeling; however, it's my responsibility regarding what I do with that emotion. It's my responsibility to figure out where it's coming from; therefore, I look at my part in the situation that caused me to have the anger. I can use our slogan "THINK" (Is it Thoughtful, Honest, Intelligent, Necessary, and Kind?) and change the angry words into something loving and kind. After I calm down, I can discuss my feelings with the other person, and hopefully I will not carry resentment as I did before working the Steps.

As a child, I'm sure I became a passive personality as a reaction to my physically and verbally abusive mother. I made a solemn vow when I became an adult that I'd never be like her; however, that passiveness created a prison in which my inner being was trapped. Because I stifled and suppressed all of my feelings, when I became an adult if someone literally "backed me into a corner" with hostile verbal or physical intent to harm me, then he/she best look out! I'd get very angry and spring into fierce action; charge with all of my strength. However, it was later suggested to me that anger in response to injustice could be healthy anger. It may be God's way of helping me protect myself.

We have a program principle: "*Expectation* is a resentment just waiting to happen." Indeed, a great reminder for me. In the past, and even now at times, I expect people to behave in a certain way: "Mary-my-way, thank you!" When they don't, resentment raises its ugly head. If I don't deal with it promptly, it will fester inside until it's much worse than when it all began.

I remember hearing one time, "It's difficult to get close to God if you are holding a resentment in your heart against one of his kids"; that made me do a lot of thinking. My heart and soul is not completely open when I'm holding resentments, since the resentment can prevent a close connection between a Higher Power and me, and my serenity.

Forgiving doesn't mean I'm a pushover today. I used to forgive my actively drinking alcoholic husband over and over. Did I really forgive him, or was I just afraid to do life on my own? Forgiveness today means I am given strength by doing that. When I forgive others, I still hold them accountable for their actions, but I take away their power to hurt me. When I resent someone, an unbreakable chain ties me to him/her, and I can't break away from the person against whom I am holding a grudge. When I decide to let go of that chain—that big hook (resentment)—then I'm ready to stop being a victim. I've decided through many years of working the Steps that forgiveness isn't about excusing bad behavior; it's about taking charge of how I myself respond to it.

I have to admit that I'm in the process of getting over a lifetime of bitterness and resentments. I was never gently touched or otherwise shown affection as a child. My reactions and avoidance of contact toward someone stretching out their hands to me were caused by memories of violence *from hands that should have been offering love.* Learning to enjoy holding someone's hand, to learn how to touch and be hugged in return in a loving, safe feeling way, had to become part of the foundation for my recovery.

I still have a small crescent scar on my thumb from an incident that occurred when I was about four years old. My mother had exploded and angrily broken a dish over my hand because I was not eating something she had made. The bitterness and sadness that resulted made me keep "treasuring" that scar so I couldn't forget the memory of that day. I kept hanging on to those emotional old, open, festering wounds until I found my spiritual support groups. They helped me forgive my mother and release those bad memories and resentments. If I hadn't, I would still be living in the past, with all of its regrets. It was suggested by other members that I tell myself over and over again: "I was a gift to my parents and a great blessing" so that I could make peace with bad memories and lay them to rest.

For years, before I came to my support group, I harbored bitterness and cynicism against my mother for the terrible way she treated me as a child, and on into most of my adult life. I used to go through many Mother's Day cards and could never find one that expressed in an honest manner my feelings about our relationship. They were all so extremely loving and complimentary and I think I was ashamed of how I truly felt about her. I always had to settle for something very short and sweet, and I felt that she was aware of that. When someone would share in a meeting how they felt about their loving mother, I felt very sad and wished I could have enjoyed a relationship with mine that way.

The last two years of my mother's life we did have a much better relationship because I accepted her just the way she was, but the love was just not there between us, and I was powerless to do anything about that. She was a terrible housekeeper, very slovenly in her appearance, and I constantly nagged and criticized her all of my life about the dirty housekeeping. I had continuously tried to get her to be a cleaner housekeeper, so I would feel more comfortable when I visited her. After I had made major changes in my perceptions and thinking, I was able to finally accept that she had a perfect right to clean her own home in whatever way she saw fit.

As an adult, I became aware that I could not expect the love from her that I offered my own daughters. I also forgave myself for not being to able to love her in a special way; however, I did give her the respect due her as my mother. With the help from using the principles in the Steps, the last few years of her life I was able to allow her to own her dignity and respect; just as I also deserved mine.

Looking back at the resentments in my marriage, I can see there were a lot of things I expected him to be or do that I could have provided for myself. Instead of "licking my wounds" and waiting for his recognition that I'd been wronged (self-pity and martyrdom, huh?), I could have been focusing on making sure that I'd get what I wanted next time, by giving those things to myself.

Even in our fellowship, I find that sometimes the words and actions of some others can make me upset and I react in my old ways of thinking and behaving. There are times when even the mere thought of a particular person disturbs my peace of mind; it can cause negative passions to arise inside me. What can I do about that? I've been told by my sponsor to ask myself, "Who's really the source of the problem?" What is not part of ourselves doesn't disturb us! What others say and do can only affect us if we allow it to. Today, I understand that as knowing *I have choices.*

The greatest resentment I had and the most difficult to overcome was toward myself. I'd beat up on Mary-Glen unmercifully and couldn't forgive her, until I put the principle of the Steps into action. Once I got it through my head that I had done the best I could with what I had been given at the time, my life began to get better, and I found peace and contentment.

Resentments are roadblocks in my path to recovery. Since working the program and letting go of them, I have more room in my soul for my Higher Power to fill up with spiritual thoughts. By forgiving others and myself I've made peace with my past. I still have to watch for expectations (premeditated resentments), for if I have certain expectations of others, or even myself, and they're not met—"ta da"—instant resentments. In my own case, if I lower my perfectionist expectations of myself to a more reasonable, attainable level, I don't set myself up to feel like a failure. Sure makes life much simpler.

While doing my Fourth Step, I also discovered I had resentment against the God *of my Understanding,* because of prayers I thought went unanswered when I was young. On bended knee, I asked Him to forgive me, and I promised I would allow Him to manage my life from now on. By doing that, He became the Power Greater Than Myself I needed and had been longing for.

Feelings of anger and resentment can be dreadful weapons; however, even though those thoughts have the ability to create hatred and scorn of others, peaceful, loving thoughts are tools of the Twelve-Step program that can be equally powerful. I try to use only those in my here and now. I find that when I offer only peace, compassion, and love, others feel that spiritual energy and are drawn to me. I attempt to use those principles daily, with God's help, and I'm now enfolded within a large family of spiritually, positive-thinking human beings. What more could I possibly want, or need? And the joy is, all of this happy balance in life began with loving myself...

My exaggerated perceptions used to have the power to interfere with the peace and harmony I longed to have in any situations I faced each day. And they still can, if I try to build a "fortress" of resentments out of a few small misunderstandings in any relationships, intimate or otherwise. My resentments today are few; if any. If one pops up, it's a lesson to be learned; I can write about it, followed by forgiveness of others and myself. Resentments can only hold me back—keep me from moving forward. Consequently, I give them to my God now, and that way I don't keep recycling them.

# 29

# *Self-esteem*

*"Don't compare your insides with other people's outsides."* *(A Twelve-Step program saying.)*

I began the process of the Twelve Steps with an awful lot of self-doubt, and those feelings had been weighing me down and keeping me from truly living for many years. In the past, I would wait for other people in the meetings to express their opinions first; that way, if mine weren't the same as theirs, I would back up and change mine. I automatically figured I must be wrong, or less informed, or whatever. If I actually believed in my mind and heart that my feelings or opinions had validity, I still held them inside and wouldn't offer my suggestions. I had such a contradictory personality in those days.

Before finding a Twelve-Step program, I didn't know this way of behaving was due to being affected by the family disease of alcoholism. I just thought I was less than others, and somehow I didn't fit in with the people around me. Thank God this program taught me that I am a worthy and beloved child of His. I also learned that there are lots of others, who feel the same way, but we have within us a great capacity to love and we learn from each other. What a wonderful feeling when I found that out. I discovered that I was not alone and that I was not less than.

I doubted all of my perceptions and myself. Some saw me as being confident and having it all together, which shows what a wonderful actress I was. The reality was that my marriage was in shambles, I was having terrifying nightmares, and I didn't know how to handle it all. *I had reached my bottom.*

I stayed with him for about six months after finding the fellowship and then *he* insisted that we had a happy life. He was happy, and I should be, also. He felt that there was nothing wrong with our marriage. It took every ounce of strength I possessed, and the support of other members, to accept my own views of my situation with him and keep coming back to the meetings. I found the strength to do that with the help of others who had walked the path before me. Without their strength, I may even have drifted back into his way of living again; even one more time.

My sponsor helped me see that I often took my perceptions of myself from the views of others, mainly my husband and my mother. If they were angry with me, then I perceived myself as having done something to deserve the anger; surely I must have done something wrong? If he/they told me that I was crazy or strange, then I believed it, no matter how much I argued or pretended not to let it bother me.

My sponsor also told me, "If he/she calls you a chair, that doesn't make you a chair, does it?" I began to see that it was my responsibility to decide my own views, attitudes, and morals, and to honor these in my actions. I also saw the burden I placed on others around me when I could not trust my views or myself. I was confused, and probably made everyone around me even more confused than I was.

I used to go to great lengths to get approval from others, and I'd temporarily feel good about myself when they'd acknowledge my contributions to their comfort, but that euphoric feeling didn't last very long. When I was alone again, I'd beat up on myself, and go back into self-loathing. Unreasonable standards of how *I should be* kept me stagnated in self-pity and low self-acceptance.

I avoided social situations because I seldom felt comfortable having conversations with others whom I felt were superior in education, financial status, and most of all in looks and social skills. I now know that those feelings of inferiority were merely *my own* lack of self-love, pride in my accomplishments, and enough confidence to trust in my inner spirit.

By working the Steps, instead of thinking negatively, I learned to view success as a possibility and another gift from God. Today, I try to dream up some realistic goals for myself; do the necessary footwork to make them successful, and leave the rest to God. The more I practice these newly found ways of building self-confidence, the more they grow.

Having self-love now means I accept and understand my true inner being and realize I am equal in social standing to all others. No one had previously taught me that I could just "Let Go and Let God" lead the way to true happiness; one small baby step at a time. Learning to value and love myself has been a deliberate, daily process with the help of the spirituality of the Twelve-Steps.

I have learned that sometimes overcoming self-doubt requires that I hold tightly to my Higher Power's hands and just step out in faith, trust in myself, and my perceptions; as the child He created. I came to believe that God would be with me through mistakes, and that mistakes are part of the process of my growth. As I grow in the program and others ask me for help, I know that I do not have all of the answers or solutions to help with their challenges; *only their Higher Power does.* If I'm unsure of how I can help them or not at all, I can tell them "Let me think about it, and I'll get back to you."

This is a program of self-love. Others loved me when I couldn't love myself and taught me how to act as if I loved and respected myself; and eventually I did. I was only a wounded person, a hurting soul, who deserved to be happy, joyous, and free. I was taught not to put my inner self down with old critical tapes; I must accept all that I am; angel wings, warts, and all.

I have my limitations like anyone else, and I don't have to pretend I am better than I am. Conversely, I don't have to make myself less than I am, either. My outer life expresses the inner me today, and what you see is what you get. I don't have to hide behind that mask; that big outward façade I had created in my battle with the disease of alcoholism. Besides which, I was told, "Masks can suffocate!" Friends helped me believe that I should never degrade myself. There are some others who will be happy to do that for me, if I don't love myself.

With help from the Steps and Slogans of this program, I slowly learned that I could like, and even love, all of my defects and myself. The loving, understanding support of my sponsor added a lot to my feelings of self-worth, as did contact with many other wonderful people in the program. I slowly realized that my self-doubt was dwindling; not gone, but a lot smaller. I know today I have the tools to help when self-doubt tries to take over my thinking process again. I like the saying I learned from my sober alcoholic husband: "Just let God control my head, and I'll control the feet."

We have four "T's" in the program: "Take Time To Think." It's often said that our thinking gets us in trouble. Well, I think it's rationalizing or justifying that causes problems in the first place. I used to do that a lot before I found Al-Anon; make excuses to cover up any of my wrongdoing, rather than admit I was wrong. Part of that type of thinking was being afraid others would use it like a weapon against me later if I admitted an error. I'm sure that was all part of the insanity of living in a home for so long where the disease runs rampant.

Through this program and a deeper relationship with the God *of my under-standing,* my sense of self-worth has grown. This all comes from listening and learning to make choices that are good for me, independent of others' views; and to care enough for myself to see that all of my needs are met. I remember early in the program, thinking of how selfish this seemed, and my religion had taught me not to be selfish. Today, I'm aware of and understand the difference.

Oh, I have further to go, that's for sure, but I think my Higher Power is allow-ing me time to get used to each new bit of self-assurance. As I feel comfortable with each new growth, He helps me uncover more things I have to work on to improve myself, and once more my lack of self-confidence shrinks a wee bit. However, I think God knows that too much at once could be overwhelming.

# 30

*Shame and Blame*

I've been told that A.A. started by one drunk saying to another, "Let's get rid of shame and find out who we really are." By the Grace of God, I'm not an alcoholic, but that is exactly what I had to do; get rid of all of the shame and blame from my past. I felt my mother and former husband continually belittled me, and feelings of unworthiness and guilt were a big part of my pre-program life. By working the Twelve Steps, I gradually learned to substitute self-love and acceptance for feelings of shame. Responsibility for myself; and personal accountability are what I need to concentrate on; not shame and blame.

Why is it so much easier to remember the actions I am ashamed of in my past? I would send myself into a "tizzy" about dumb things I had said or done in the past that had embarrassed me, and I bet I'm the only one that remembers them. I had to go back into my childhood and give my inner child all of the love and support she felt she had never been given. When I felt sadness from all of those years of shame and blame, I let the healing tears flow. Today, I am aware that many times feelings of shame are not from anything I've done in the past; *but rather they are from someone else's verbal abuse against me.*

When I became an adult, I blamed my mother and husband for my negative way of thinking, self-pity, and general outlook on life. I finally ended that habit of blaming others for my own lack of responsibility for my actions and behavior, and gave up justifying and qualifying my mistakes or reactions.

As a child, because of my penurious parents, I was always dressed in bad-looking second-hand clothes and ill-fitting shoes. My mother was an extremely lazy housekeeper, and had bad personal hygiene. She was also a miser, by choice, and would not spend the proverbial penny on *anything* if she could possibly avoid it.

Therefore, I always felt ashamed about my appearance; especially compared to other middle-class youngsters.

After a lot of reflection about my past, I concluded that my mother became a miser and denied the family even the simplest materialistic necessities because she had been very poor as a youngster and had set a goal of accumulating a million dollars in savings. I can understand that all now as being her way of establishing her own self-worth. (If she had lived a few years longer, she'd have made that particular goal.) I give her credit, though, for putting a tremendous effort into becoming a "life master" at bridge, and I do admire her for that. My feeble attempts to find feelings of self-worth as an adult were by having a nice home and other material things, because I wasn't yet aware that my self-worth had to *begin on the inside.*

All of that shame and blame is in the past and cannot be undone, but this is my here and now. I live to love and enjoy who I am today; the unique special lady God had planned I'd become, if the cruel disease of alcoholism hadn't affected me. Outside stuff does not define inside stuff. Before recovery began I had lost my self; I became what others told me I was! Today, I wonder, "Why would anyone want to let others control their thoughts and feelings?" Maybe to be told what a "good girl" I was, or what a "good wife" I was? Well, phooey with those old ideas; I am worthy today just because I am!

As a child, I believed that I had to earn worthiness through what I did and how I behaved. If I did nice things for you, then I thought you'd love me. I tried unceasingly to be what you wanted me to be. As I grew up, I was treated, or felt I was, as if what I did was never good enough in other's eyes to be acceptable. I used to wait for things to maybe go away or expect that others would solve my problems for me and make everything "all better." The program has taught me that those who have already worked the program before me can offer me solutions that have worked for them, but no one else can do the actual resolving for me. I have to take responsibility for my own life and stop blaming others for wherever I happen to be in the moment; physically or emotionally.

I can admire, love, and respect qualities in others in the program without any clue to their past—love them just as they are now—and that's exactly what I had to learn to do *for myself.* Self-exploration in working the Steps helped me find all of my attributes and I can focus on those qualities now. I deserve all good things I receive from God, just being who I am, and just as I am. I believe now that I am totally 100% acceptable and loveable; 100% of the time. Period! That's it!

Today I value my own thoughts and feelings. I will never again let anyone shame and blame me and take away my dignity and self-respect, and I'll keep myself my #1 priority; after God, of course. I don't have to accept blame from others or cast shame back at them. I try my best not to get into heated discussions about whose fault it is. Instead, I try to focus on the problem itself; and what solution is best for my own comfort and the others involved. When I do that, my loved ones are also rewarded.

# 31

## *Sponsorship and Sharing our Experience, Strength, and Hope*

*Someone in the program put this well: "A sponsor is a friend who knows you as you are, understands where you've been, accepts who you're becoming, and still gently invites you to grow." (Author unknown)*

I need to feel accountable to someone—oftentimes on a daily basis—and that means staying in touch with someone I know, trust, and feel that they care about me. Usually that comes with an intimate relationship with a sponsor, or it can also be simply by picking up the telephone and calling someone on the group 'phone list that I respect and trust; and feel safe enough with to share whatever is troubling me.

I knew I couldn't work the Steps in a meaningful way without a sponsor. I greatly admired one younger woman who: looked great, was extremely self-confident, shared at meetings, had serenity, was of service at the group level, always seemed to suggest just the right solution for the problems, and exactly at the proper time. *Something was working in her life, and I wanted what she had.*

One evening after a meeting she gave me some great program suggestions about a challenge that I thought could really work for me, so I spontaneously asked her to sponsor me. She agreed, however, she explained that she didn't yet know what we had in common; and that we could have the sponsorship relationship on a trial basis. By doing that, if one of us felt the mentoring was not working, we could say so and there would be no hurt feelings. It turned out to be a great sponsor/sponsee relationship for me.

She listened to me very intently while I cried a lot and told her my problem. She asked questions that led me to a greater understanding of my situation. She never gave me advice, but shared her own experience and taught me to think differently. Together, we'd work out the challenge. By the end of each conversation with her, I was in a much better place emotionally, and I had the spiritual tools of Al-Anon I needed for dealing with the situation on my own.

At first the former people pleaser in me did many of the things she suggested, just to win her approval. I admired her so much, I would have gone to any lengths she suggested to ease my emotional pain. Eventually the program kicked in for me, and I understood the reasons for her suggestions and the reasons why we had to do the Steps in order with a sponsor. She also emphasized that I had to study the Twelve Steps, the Twelve Traditions, and Twelve Concepts of the program horizontally, which made me better informed at meetings, as well as a more loving, contributing member of my own family. She later encouraged me to start doing service at the group level and beyond, which also became a major contributor to my growth.

A sponsor does not necessarily have all of the answers because she is merely another human being who is recovering from the effects of someone's addiction. None of us is finished with our personal growth, no matter how long we have been working the program. A sponsor helps me find my own answers—in my own time—and she is always there for me when I need her. Most of the time she knows what I'm feeling before I can verbalize those feelings myself. She helps me laugh at myself and feel loved, unconditionally.

Life went smoothly. My sponsor worked with me on changing my attitudes, tone of voice, and behavior and led me to begin to apply the Twelve-Step principles in all my affairs so that it would simply become a way of life. After about three years in the program, I began to sponsor newcomers myself whenever they asked me. To this day, I seldom, if ever, turn anyone down. A mentor told me that if someone asks me if I have time to sponsor her because she feels I seem to be a very busy person, I could tell her, "I always have a need for one more than God has given me."

My understanding of the Steps, Traditions, and Concepts of Service grows as these women challenge me to walk with them in order to overcome the effects that the devastating disease of alcoholism has had on their lives simply by living with it. Today I see my role as a sponsor as being able to convince someone of their own self-worth, and that self-love will empower them to solve their own problems after working the Twelve Steps.

I think in sponsoring, and in our meetings, when another human being shares their innermost thoughts about how he/she handles the frustration and challenges of life, it helps us understand what choices we have to deal with in a similar situation. We can use their experiences like a spiritual source of wisdom. I believe now that God does work through others' lives to help each one of us.

I became aware, through the years, that true humility helps me share what I have to offer—and what I am right now—without waiting until I have something eloquent or profound to share. When each member shares in meetings, I am free to pick and choose whatever seems most useful for my own emotional growth, and then to disregard the rest. By sharing in meetings, I've also learned to be honest and open with my loved ones, instead of continuing to take their inventory. What a blessing that is now, and I try to make my home feel to others as I do in meetings, i.e. full of safety and nurturing.

Sharing my own human side and being honest about my fears, hurts, sadness, anger, weariness, and occasional doubts about my faith helps others also share any difficulties they may encounter in the program. Sometimes, when I feel I am falling apart, getting those feelings all out in a meeting is how I put myself back together. I've also overcome a lot of hazards along the way by doing that. With the help of sponsors and other members who work a lot at their Twelve Steps, I am learning to express my own soul.

In the program, we are a very diverse group of people with a common purpose, and I humbly believe the power of words can almost miraculously motivate others to find their own solutions to challenges. For a while, negative things were being shared in a meeting I had attended for a long time. I discussed this with my sponsor and she graciously pointed out to me that it sounded as if I were picking out only the things I objected to, didn't like, and ignoring the positive elements I needed for my own recovery.

With her help, I have determined that while in a meeting I can only share my own experience, strength, and hope, and keep my feet on the path that is best for me. Somehow, when I do that, I find I can trust others to do the same, and the miracle of mutual assistance is evident to me once more. As I continue on in my Twelve-Step pathway, I begin to see more and more often that there is a spiritual renewal at every meeting I attend, and I can either respond to that Spirit or close it out of my life. Today, I choose to participate fully in my meetings and let others work their program as they see fit.

On the sad day of September 11, when the Twin Towers were destroyed, about twenty minutes before my regular meeting a sponsee called me and told me to turn on the TV and we heard the dreadful news. My feelings went back to the horrors of growing up in World War Two in Europe, and I cried when I saw the Twin Towers disintegrating before my eyes. I asked God to help everyone involved, and I said a prayer for those suffering; then my husband reminded me of our program saying, "Continue with what you were doing when this terrible thing happened," which can be applied to any circumstances.

We went to our meeting and most of the regular members were there, which I did not expect. (I had been afraid that no one would show up, and if they did, that all of the discussion would be about the disastrous news.) Instead, we had our usual topics from our two daily program meditation books, talked a lot about strength and wisdom from a Power Greater Than Ourselves, and carried on with our lives "Just for today." We knew we were powerless, but God was with us.

I thank God daily for the women who had the fortitude to start our Twelve-Step program many years ago and hung in there with it, in spite of lots of hardships and challenges in the beginning. Their sponsorship, spirituality and love continue on in the program today, and without them, I would not be living the beautiful life I now have.

# 32

# *Stumbling Blocks into Stepping Stones*

God is often described as the potter and we are the clay. I believe He installed my Spirit and molded me, using His own big plan for my identity in life, but my life's experiences helped change me into the personality I was before I found this great fellowship.

In the healing Steps, I pictured myself sitting on my path to recovery with a big sign in front of me, "Under Construction," and I was surrounded by many stumbling blocks; almost buried in them. They were roadblocks that held me back from moving on in recovery and serenity. I believe my Power Greater is slowly helping me by removing some of them and by making me more aware when I use them. I want to become a person who will bring true joy and happiness to any relationship I am in—intimate or otherwise—and I believe that by praying "Thy will be done" instead of my way be done, God is giving me an internal transformation (a little remodeling job!). But there are still, even after many years of working the Twelve Steps, lots of stumbling blocks in my way which have to be removed before I can achieve that state of bliss. God loves me as I am; however, He knows there is lots of room for improvement.

With the help of these Steps, I'm discovering my bona fide inner-self under all of the garbage I had stuffed on top of it before I began the program, due to my inability to tell my former husband, or anyone else for that matter, what I was really feeling. By dumping all of the bad stuff, I was able to write out the thoughts flowing from my heart and soul, and I learned many things about my own inner being by doing that. I've been self-improving since beginning the program, and I'll continue to be under construction until my Higher Power thinks I'm finished. I'm becoming my precious new self, and no one else can do that for me.

I am a recovering perfectionist. My biggest stumbling block can still be perfectionism; I can still go there. Alcoholics know where "there" is for them—it's any old drinking environment; and "there" for me is old stinking thinking and behavior from the disease. Today, I am aware when I have handled a situation much better than I ever could have before Al-Anon, and I am grateful for that improvement in all of my relationships.

In the beginning, perfectionism kept me from sharing what I truly wanted to share; I thought I had to wait until I had something truly profound and eloquent before I shared with others. The first few months I recited—parroted—whatever I read in the program literature; however, I wasn't actualizing it in my daily life and relationships. When I began dropping my ridiculous perfectionist standards, I began to share my truths from my inner Spirit, and I slowly began to heal. Besides which, I discovered that *humility and my truths* earned me more love and respect from others than *any* perfectionist standards ever had. My goal is to let the light from my inner Spirit shine through in everything I say or do.

The stumbling blocks have led me to use slogans as stepping-stones; therefore our slogan, "Keep It Simple," is becoming a constant reminder to me that my best is good enough. With this principle in mind, I can appreciate the little steps I have taken to reach a much more sensible, happier way of life. I'm also learning not to make everything I do into such a big deal, and actually start to enjoy more of what I'm doing, whether in my writing, practicing my piano, or my housework.

# 33

## *Support and Unconditional Love from Others*

My Twelve-Step program is based in the heart; my heart reaches out to your heart in compassion to help with the healing process. I don't need a degree or job title to do that. I need support, true humility, and willingness to give and receive experience, strength, and hope. I no longer have to feel and/or be isolated; I only have to open myself to the support that is all around me in the Fellowship.

We are all equal in a Twelve-Step program, and that thought makes me feel comfortable. There are no "experts" in our group meeting rooms, and even if some of the people in the meeting are professionals in their day-to-day careers, they come to the Twelve-Step meetings as fellow members. When I attend a meeting, even if I don't know anyone in the room, I can leave any insecurity I may have been feeling outside because inside that room are people just like me who will accept me just as I am, and who understand where I'm coming from. What a wonderful feeling to know they won't judge me or criticize my speech, and that is something one doesn't often find. Consequently, I am able to share from the heart and make myself vulnerable, yet not feel uncomfortable doing that.

Other members can understand me in a way that others outside the program cannot. No one judges, lectures, or gives advice; rather they share from their experience and their hearts. They don't need a textbook to understand what it's like to live with the effects of alcoholism. They already know, because they live, or have lived with, the actual experience. I believe that a living, human survivor and example is my *best teacher.*

I became aware that many of my coping mechanisms were inappropriate. I tried to keep the family together, and I shielded our daughters from as much unpleasantness as possible. I negated my own needs, feeling that to attend to them would be selfish, and rushed around doing everything for everyone else. Most of the time I felt very depressed and couldn't see a way out. My Al-Anon groups saved me from that way of living. It was so comforting to know that there were others who had suffered the same fear, anger, confusion and frustration I had gone through; people in whom I could safely confide and trust.

I humbly pray that God will always keep me from sounding like I am lecturing or acting like a self-proclaimed expert in my meetings or otherwise. I alone don't have the answers for others' difficulties, but together we have all of the answers, with the help of a Power Greater. I believe I am responding to His love for me—and within me—when I show another human being love, kindness, empathy, or an understanding heart. There will always be families and friends of alcoholics who need the experience, strength, and hope of members like me, and the love and support that comes from our basic human need of community, which we find in an Al-Anon, support group.

When I first came into the program, I'd call my sponsor with a complaint about my active alcoholic and her standard remark was: "And what was your part in that?" I didn't really understand her question at first, until I was in a meeting on Step Four one evening and I heard someone say that one of their character defects was that they always approached problems from a "victim's role." That was exactly what I'd been doing, without realizing it. With the support of other members, God's help, and my sponsor, I began to change that attitude and start facing my problems, using a survivor's role instead of the poor me approach. That meant I didn't need to be given sympathy, but had boundaries that I expected to be respected.

I needed to depend on the support of other members to help me learn how to set boundaries. After years of trying to cope on my own, I was too enmeshed with his bad emotions to be able to think for myself. Fear of being alone kept me in that marriage, and fear of not being able to support myself financially. I can see now that fear controlled me, and I actually lacked the courage to take care of my own welfare. Once I opened up my heart and soul to my support groups, I learned that I had other sources of love in this world, and God was providing them. I was no longer alone or had to suffer from feelings of fear.

I relied on the experience and insights of other Al-Anons to stand up against the feelings of guilt created by old video and audio tapes, which had imprisoned me for so long—not let them control me—and stop recycling them. I learned to take care of my own interests: emotionally, financially, and spiritually.

Today I know I can set boundaries; I have choices, and I can make decisions for my own welfare. I thank God every day for that spiritual growth enlightenment. My support groups hold me up and make sure I keep my feeling of well being, and they are always there for me.

# 34

# *The Need to Be Right Can Slowly Destroy a Relationship*

Before working the Twelve Steps with a sponsor, I thought there were only two ways to think: Mary-my-way, and the wrong way!

I began being a mature responsible adult when I could cheerfully accept the fact that I am not always "right." Then my mind became open to receiving the helpful insights I am given in our literature, in our meetings, and from my Higher Power. I 'm now convinced that an *extreme need to be right* has the power to destroy any relationships with others, intimate or otherwise.

Beginning in childhood, I think I developed that need as one of my self-protective mechanisms. I wanted everyone to be loving and kind around me, and I kept trying to make him/her that way. I used to tell my first husband, "You should read this; it's great." He'd respond, "No, you read it; *you* need it." Oh well…I thought that whatever I read in one of my many self-help books just had to be the *right* answer for me and everyone else I connected with. I guess you might say I definitely had a closed mind.

I diligently began to change that need to be right by meditating and writing down guidance from my Power Greater Than Myself. I've now accepted that my perceptions—my own unique way of seeing things and life as it flows around me—are all the result of personal experiences and teachings I internalized from others.

A mentor of mine in the program gave me a metaphor one time about my perceptions; they are like the lens in glasses that are made to the special needs of my eyes. She said, "It would be unusual that the lens made to fit your eyesight would work for someone else. Therefore, you have to remember that we each *see* people, places, and situations differently at times." That doesn't mean that what I see is right and that you are wrong. I'm also becoming aware that the longer I work on changing my attitudes and behavior, the more my perceptions also change. It's an ever, ongoing process.

At one time, I thought that every problem required a solution, that every argument just had to be resolved by agreement on both sides, and one of us had to give in. I'd argue and discuss, fight it out if I had to; as if it were "charge, the battle must be won!" I know today that sometimes it means there's not complete agreement on an issue; it means that I am content with my own feelings, and must allow others to be content with theirs.

I like living this principle today: You can have your ideas and I can have mine. Agreeing to disagree brings peace and harmony to all of my relationships. What a great feeling to know that I don't have to battle with others; it's just not worth the time and energy it takes to feel that I am right. I can easily diffuse a heated discussion by using the simple program saying, "You may be right," and walk away; however, it's not always appropriate. For example, my ex-alcoholic husband used to say, "Oh, you're so selfish." I've since been taught in the program that's just another way of saying, "Do it my way!"

A lot of my unnecessary need to feel right came from a lifetime of living with the active disease He always had to feel that he was right, and I just had to challenge him, of course. I think he also had to try to feel he was right to make up for his feelings of inadequacy and low self-esteem. I lived with constant verbal abuse and "chop down" type of humor. When I communicated something with him, one of his favorite games was to immediately say, "I don't think so." One day I woke up and told him, "put a period after *think*." He repeated that slowly and then said, "Oh, you're getting smart!" It was then I realized he'd been saying that all of those years just to get me angry. Good example of insane behavior, on my part.

When I disagree with something someone says or does, anger can creep in if I allow that to happen. Before working the Steps I'd try to show that person, by whatever jumped into mind, that my way and opinion was best. That would create tension, and probably harmed some relationships along the way. Nowadays, if someone is displaying thinking or behavior that is unacceptable to me, I can easily say, "I don't feel comfortable with that."

I choose to have peace and harmony in my relationships today. My point of view now means it matters very little if I don't agree with your perspectives of whatever the problem is at the moment. I can stop and think, "How Important Is

It" or will it be a year from now; or even twenty-four hours from now? That's why I like to tell those I sponsor, when they have a challenge facing them, "just wait twenty-four hours." I take care of my own wants and needs today; but I am not a self-centered person. In fact, sometimes I can still be too generous with my time and money to my own detriment. Only more years in the program will take care of that challenge. At least I know today that I am not "self-less."

I've been an avid reader since a very young age; I escaped reality that way when I lived with active alcoholism. I seldom watched TV, and I still don't, but I would check out about a dozen non-fiction books from the library about every two weeks. (Most of them were self-improvement books.) I worked on myself, but I think I was really trying to self-improve him. (Of course, that didn't work either.) I escaped the problems of an active alcoholic marriage by constantly reading, and I thought that whatever I read in one of my many books just had to be the right answer. Today, with the help of my daily Tenth Step Inventory, I can make sure that being opinionated—which I think of also as "the need to be right"—does not creep back into my daily conversations and interactions with all others.

One of my miracles today is that when I recognize that I am using my old behavior of feeling that I am *right,* I can take the risk of walking away from a situation rather than *righting it,* according to my perspectives. The miracle by doing that is that I feel free to be me today, because I am using what I have been taught in the program: I have a right to an opinion; however, you have a perfect right to have yours. And, I don't have to make someone else's situation right—it belongs to them.

Paul taught me in our relationship to say "I agree with you," rather than "You are right," because that way we are reminded that neither of us is right. After all, it's really not about who is right; its about what is right, and only God knows what is right. Today we try to keep the slogan "How Important Is It?" uppermost in our minds and relationships.

# 35

## *Trusting Myself and Others*

I have great peace with my past today because my perspectives of abuse from others have changed to one of forgiveness; however, I had suffered a lifetime with no trust in anyone before I found Al-Anon.

My early experience about trust was the program slogan, "Let It Begin With Me." I first had to learn to accept myself just as I am and trust my own intuitions. I believe the depth of my inner soul is where my Higher Power speaks to me. I found one meaning of *trust* in my dictionary to be "a confident expectation." I think that's a great definition. If I take enough time every day to spend with Him and listen for His voice, I will have the right guidance and wisdom to believe in myself, but I had to practice doing that before I could trust and believe in anyone else.

My view of spirituality began to change as I began to heal. This really started with the love and care of a good sponsor who taught me to take on the awesome responsibility of self-care. Eventually, I had enough healing that I could really self-examine my life and feelings with honesty.

I discovered that as a result of living with the disease and all that goes along with it, I had come to distrust that God *could or would* intervene in my life and give me His support. I felt that I had many unanswered prayers in my lifetime, and had almost given up hope for help from God.

One of those experiences was when my ex-husband admitted himself to a treatment center for about six weeks; about two years before we ultimately separated. That evening I told my prayer group I felt I had just received a miracle: he was going to be sober and we could begin a new life together. (I had never told them, or others for that matter, of the ongoing problems with alcoholism.)

The night after he was released from the hospital, I went home from my prayer meeting and found the front door locked. We seldom locked the doors in our part of town. (Besides which, we had an unusually large Airdale terrier that would have scared anyone away.) When I rang the doorbell, he opened it for me and his speech was slurred and he was "weaving" on his feet. I used a typical Al-Anon response to the situation and said, "Tell me you're joking. You're not drunk, are you?" But he was. The disease had won. It was cunning, baffling and, once again, had destroyed my hope for a better life.

I was too ashamed, humiliated, and embarrassed to go back and confess to the prayer group what had occurred. I asked God, "Why did this have to happen?" I felt as if He had also failed me. Toward the final closure of our marriage, I even felt God had also abandoned me somewhat. Of course He hadn't; I was just lost in my own misery. I think that is one of the reasons I spent two years on the first three steps, trying to make sure I applied them to my daily life. I had to learn to trust: first God, then myself, and then other Al-Anons.

I can't have acceptance in my life without having the humility to surrender control of my way to my Higher Power. Everything that flows into my life on a daily basis is under His control. Today I don't have to be in the midst of a beautiful outdoor setting created by Him, or even a church building in His honor, to feel His presence in my life. I only need to open my eyes and ears to receive the messages from God that come in many different forms and ways, and be more aware of the miracles that continuously happen almost on a daily basis.

Before working the Steps, I never slowed down, took enough time out to listen to the voice of my inner Spirit. I was too busy focusing on others and letting them act is if they were my Higher Power. This program has changed that insanity. Instead of asking Him to make my life better, I learned to ask *what His will might be for me.* In so many wonderful ways, my relationship with God has deepened by doing that.

I developed a strong religious faith in God, beginning in my childhood, by listening to and putting into practice what I learned from others. I am following centuries of traditions and beliefs of people who have gone before me and walked in God's light. I take what I like in my religion and I leave the rest for others. Today I feel that way about our Al-Anon Program. At first I didn't understand or have faith that the Twelve Steps could lead me to serenity, peace and harmony in my life until I saw proof with my own eyes that the people who had walked the Twelve-Step recovery path before me had that happy balance in their lives. I was able to put my trust in them to show me the way, and they have never failed me.

I may not always like where the will of my Power Greater takes me; nevertheless, if I keep Him as the center of my life, I know I can handle whatever comes my way. Sometimes it's humanly difficult to remember to do that, but practice means growth. I know now that I must always have my personal slogan uppermost in my mind, "God is the Center of My Life," and not let anyone or anything else replace Him in that position. My priorities are as follows: first, God and my program, because He *is my* program; second, myself; third, my loved ones.

Today I know that God is the: *who, the what, and the where* that can and will help me through this; therefore, He is where I place my trust and where I look for guidance and comfort. This particular gift of principles is such a miracle for me; I have something that helps me feel safe and serene. This program is truly a spiritual awakening, if I just "Let Go and Let God" work in my life, and I now believe that *a spiritual awakening is a cumulative process of working the Twelve Steps.*

Loving people in our meetings taught me to be gentle with myself. They told me it was okay to make mistakes, and I'm allowed to do that because I'm only human. As a result of working the Twelve Steps and being surrounded by people who encouraged and understood me, I slowly began to heal from the old wounds and doubts. Little by little I began to see the gifts that God has given me. (A Twelve-Step acronym for GIFT is God Is Forever There.) I began to see myself in a healthier way, both my good and bad qualities, and my confidence started to grow.

Trust in my Higher Power took time. I attended meetings and found that I could trust my Home Group. I found a sponsor I felt I could trust completely. Finally, it occurred to me that my Higher Power was working through the people I trusted, so why not put my trust in that Power Greater whom I have always known as God. Many, many days at a time have allowed me to build a trusting relationship with a Higher Power who loves me unconditionally. I'm learning never to let one road end without finding a new one that God is making for me; to look for new challenges, and to keep working on self-discovery, regardless of how old I am. I plan to keep working the Twelve-Steps daily, finding new and exciting things to do with my life until God takes me on to life eternal.

I love the saying I memorized many years ago: "Faith is knowing that when I come to the end of the light and I leap into the darkness, I will have solid ground to land on or I'll be given wings to fly." (Author anonymous)

Whatever my needs are today, I trust God enough to give them to Him in prayer, and then I listen and wait for His response. Many times His answer may be in something I unexpectedly hear someone share in a meeting, or a passage in a book I pick up at random, but mainly it comes from my soft loving voice in my inner spirit and soul—my Power Greater Than Myself.

# 36

# *Turning Negatives into Positives*

*"Happiness indicates I have a positive state of mind." (Author unknown)*

I think a Twelve-Step program offers principles that help us change our old stinking (negative) thinking into positive emotionally healthy ways of looking at life and its challenges.

In the past, especially while living with the active disease, I did a lot of emotional runaways and geographic moves away from challenges. Looking at those emotionally unhealthy solutions for problems from a distance now, I'm able to understand that doing that type of behavior only gave the people, places, and state of affairs I was running from—*more power over me.* I used to carry such a big burden of discontent with things, as they were, that I couldn't see where I was or where I was heading. Today, I face a problem head on. I am aware of it, and I accept it with the reality of what it is worth. I look for healthy ways of solving it, with God's help of course, and that keeps me from being negative toward current happenings.

My negative self-talk, previous to joining my fellowship, was detrimental to my emotional stability. I began by posting positive affirmations on my mirror so my brain would get retrained to keep on a positive path. I'd lived a life of negative self-abuse when I came to the recovery rooms, and gradually I began to discover, understand, and love the special person I was in God's eyes. I had to polish up my self-image mirror that my sponsor held up to show me, and wipe off all of the negative messages I was sending myself. In that way, I came to appreciate our program saying: "God doesn't make junk."

I did a lot of bookkeeping when I was young. I have very good penmanship and that was important in bookkeeping, long before computers took over. I thought about it recently; a negative could be turned into a positive in those days by a simple stroke of a pen. Emotionally, it's not that simple; however, I'm learning that I don't have to make myself feel guilty because someone in a relationship (intimate or otherwise) is having a bad day. If they are in a miserable, grouchy mood, I don't have to absorb that attitude. I believe that I create the atmosphere around me, so I can let them have their feelings and still make my day a great one.

I'd like to think that before working the Twelve Steps I was a positive thinker, but I only thought I was. Instead, my life was like an old vaudeville routine a mentor shared with me that plays out like this: "My husband is ruining my life," sobbed the young wife." "Now dear," said the friend, "Let's try to be positive about things." "Oh, okay," said the wife, "I'm positive he's ruining my life!" My mentor, and that old story, helped me change that particular way of thinking.

In my heart I truly felt I had gone past Step One when I became part of my first support group. I had spent a lifetime fighting the battle with his alcoholism and trying to fix him, and all to no avail. I definitely knew I was powerless over alcohol. My life was such a mess, and it was unmanageable. I had the mistaken illusion that all I had to do was have this program show me a few quick fixes, after which I was convinced I could live my life happily ever after.

It did not take me long to learn that this program was not going to fix the alcoholic in my life, nor would I be able to. There was a lot of work I had to do on myself to bring some sanity into my then chaotic life. In the program we say: "We don't "listen to learn," we "learn to listen!" In my case, listening for the simple reason that I had stuffed my feelings all of my life and never shared them with anyone else; learning, because when I sat quietly long enough, something was sure to bring me enlightenment.

When I listened and learned, I came to understand that I had been ruining my own life by staying in the negative, constantly whining about what that devastating disease had done to my life. When I decided to "Live and Let Live," I was free to see that by thinking positively my perceptions of people and circumstances changed in many ways. By changing my distorted thinking, I could see that without any doubt I had been a good person, good mother, and good wife to my ex-husband. Most importantly, by thinking positively—instead of the down side—things were getting even better, all the way around

Verbal abuse can take many forms. It can really hurt, if I allow it to. Joking criticism is one; it can be a put down. I feel it can also destroy a relationship because my reactions turn into blame and resentment. I know now that I don't have to do that. I can respond with a positive statement to counteract the negative one, whether from inside myself or from someone else, then serenely go about my day. The program has taught me that I am responsible for whatever words I feed my subconscious.

I've worked my way through many broken promises and shattered dreams. I've felt that part of my heart was being been torn apart, but with others' help I've grown spiritually. I depended on my Higher Power and the fellowship to get me through it all. Now I am learning to face circumstances or a relationship the way it really is, not how I wish that it could be.

People in the program often ask me how I managed to survive that marriage for so long. I think I actually was using some positive principles of the program prior to finding a support group for families and friends of alcoholics. I always wanted to be a pianist, but was never given the opportunity to do so. Therefore, I got a beautiful console piano and proceeded to practice it about four hours per day; that was after I had reached my fiftieth birthday. I had resigned my employment then, for I thought it would help our relationship if he didn't have much pressure on him to help with work on our homes. I decided later, that was a big mistake on my part as it only made me feel more subservient and dependent on him, and he made sure I was aware of that fact every opportunity he got. Nevertheless, I detached from his disease and obsessed about the piano! The gift from doing that was I became, after many years, an accomplished pianist,.

A few months after I retired, God had a wonderful surprise for me. My older daughter had remarried and thought she wouldn't be able to get pregnant, but God had other plans. On hearing the news that she was expecting to have a baby after all, guess who was the first to offer to baby-sit fulltime so she could continue working? *Why Mary-Glen, the future grandma, of course...*Taking care of my precious grandbaby helped me detach from the alcoholic. It also helped form a strong bond with my granddaughter, and we dearly love each other.

When I gave up my career, I missed all of the children and parents I helped by working as the only secretary in a school office with several hundred students; therefore, babysitting with her proved to be the bridge of transition I needed to keep me from feeling I was no longer needed, or that I was unnecessary to society. That was just another experience that proved to me that there are definitely no coincidences in my life; *it is all part of God's plan.*

I taught myself sewing and other crafts, and I did a lot of retail therapy during that period; however, like many of us, I became a loner when I lived with his active disease because all of the hobbies I chose were performed alone. I was isolated from social contacts and felt as if I had nowhere to fit in. I had acquaintances, but no special friends to confide in, and there was never any meaningful communication with my husband—by his choice. I can now see that isolation is an escape, a much easier path to use rather than facing reality.

Looking back, I am aware now that negativity kept my life at a complete standstill. Negative attitudes kept me from living a hope-filled, joyous life; one that God wants every human being to have. Instead I am challenged now to find positive qualities in other human beings, my circumstances, and myself. Working the Steps helped me discover valuable positive attributes about my own self that I could work on instead of concentrating on the negative aspects of others.

No matter how many years I'm in the program, I will always be in a continuous process of relieving myself of self-pity thoughts by changing them to a strong, tolerant way of thinking and behaving. Others taught me that I had choices and I could prolong my misery by continuing with old, damaging, behaviors, or I could replace them with more positive actions that would help improve my relationships—intimate or otherwise. Positive actions and behavior for me today include having gratitude and contentment with all of my blessings from God.

# 37

## *Vulnerability*

To be "vulnerable," according to the dictionary, means "capable of or susceptible to being wounded or hurt physically or emotionally." I have looked under this topic in our program literature, and haven't been able to find anything, in the index or otherwise; yet it is a subject that I feel is an integral part of the program. Most of us come to the program with not much trust in anyone or anything.

My actively drinking alcoholic used a lot of ridicule jokes directed toward me that I felt were extremely hurtful. If I complained, he would say, "Oh, you are just too sensitive." I have since learned in the program that verbal banter is used a lot by a practicing alcoholics; however, that type of chop down humor is not hilarious in any way to the people it is aimed it. It is sarcasm, and sarcasm comes from a word meaning "to tear flesh." I'm convinced that sort of humor should be left to standup comics in the nightclub bars.

Our friends, or maybe I should call them "acquaintances," were mainly actively drinking alcoholics, since they were of his choosing; consequently, I suffered through a lot of that type of humor. One of the reasons I love the good-natured laughter in the rooms of our Twelve-Step program is that they are good-natured remarks made at our own expense, and no one else's. We know we are well on the way to recovery when we can laugh at our mistakes.

Before working the Twelve Steps, I didn't want to continue being hurt by someone's words or actions, so I learned to be cynical and disbelieving, not only of him, but also of others. This was part of the pattern of my life; when someone hurt me, I would add to the protective wall I had built around myself. I didn't like feeling vulnerable, so I isolated, wore my false façade, and didn't trust anyone. I shut out everything—even the good in others—in my efforts to escape the emotional pain of it all.

That is why it took me such a long time to open up to others. I greatly admire newcomers who can embrace the program and start to grow and bloom right away, but that was not the case for me. Though I didn't trust the groups as a whole, after awhile I slowly began to let my defenses down to individuals; and I willingly began seeking to establish a connection to a Power Greater Than Myself. Sometimes my voice, hands, and my knees would tremble when I tried to share myself with others (and occasionally that still happens today), but the only way I could get well was to render myself vulnerable to something or someone that would never take advantage of my trust; to take that risk of being loved unconditionally. By doing that, I eventually accepted that the rooms of a Twelve-Step program were a safe refuge in which to share and bare my inner being.

The inflammatory words and actions of others, if they're aimed at me now, just bounce off me and no longer hurt. Other long time members taught me that someone's words and actions could only hurt me, if I allowed that to happen. If someone was unkind or thoughtless, I had the option not to take it personally. By not obsessing about keeping a mental record of others' hurtful words and actions now, I usually don't notice them. This is a precious gift that has made my life more peaceful and given me a more positive outlook on life. I'm also learning that being vulnerable is a huge blessing; it can lead to intimacy in any relationship. The closeness with others that my soul always hungered for is possible when I am no longer afraid of being wounded.

There's an old adage (author unknown), "It is our vulnerability and weakness that binds us, not our strength." My vulnerability is being able to share myself honestly in our groups and admit my shortcomings, and it is others expressing the same thing that tells me I am not alone. A program mentor I admire likes to share in meetings that: "We need to render ourselves vulnerable to this program before we can get well." I try to follow that suggestion now. Trusting people in the meetings and being able to share my deepest inner being with them helps me practice being genuine in my personal relationships.

After many years in Al-Anon, I'm convinced that a close relationship with a loved one means that I have to share my true inner being and not play sick games. When I developed enough love and trust in myself and others, I was able to show them my true self so that they would also know me; who I am and what I'm truly about. Today, if I begin a relationship with someone that I hope to develop and cherish, (especially in sponsorship) I want to try to help him/her understand the sadness of my past, my fears, my secrets, and invite him/her to participate in my life and recovery.

In intimate relationships, there are times when people *unintentionally* make mistakes that may hurt one another, but when both people work their own Twelve-Steps programs, they can develop a very beautiful relationship. *I am in one of those today with my beloved, and we have the blessing of a Power Greater Than Myself.*

For the past few years I have been working on living my life in a much more meaningful way. I want to do all the things I can possibly plan and dream of in the years I may have left in this lifetime, but I can find a million reasons why I think I won't be able to bring those to a successful conclusion. The only reason I can offer is *fear*. I worry that perhaps I will become vulnerable to someone else's thinking and perceptions of "she's too old to do that" or "what I did or did not do right."

I can't truly live my life to its fullest if I am afraid to open up and show others the genuine me, and in that respect, just writing this book has definitely been a challenge and has taken a lot of courage. I believe that is where our Higher Power and the Twelve Steps help us; they truly give us the strength to become great human beings; *at least in our eyes and His. That is another miracle of the program for me.*

In a spiritual program, we all need to concentrate on helping others by sharing our lives with them in a completely authentic manner. Today, I am positive that sharing my story, my example of thinking and behaving (and also that of other members), is more convincing that the program *does work;* even more so than studying our literature. I do have faith in our literature, *but I feel that human contact is invaluable.* It is only communicated member to member by each one sharing his/her own story and/or a problem—face to face—that they have found the solution to by using the program principles.

When I am willing to share in a meeting about an event I'm deeply ashamed of (like an incident I may have been trying to keep secret most of my life), if I want to help someone else, I have to be straightforward about my own life. It's my honesty that inspires others to change. I don't want to continue to live in the problems of the past; when I live in the solution, there is no problem. Because of a lack of trust in God, in some others, and even in myself, there was a time when I was afraid to appear vulnerable—afraid I'd be used and betrayed. Today I can allow others to come into my life and unconditionally love them, whether or not they return the sentiment.

I'm also convinced that the people in the program who are the most emotionally healthy are the ones who are not afraid of being vulnerable. They share their most intimate inner feelings and beliefs in such an honest open way; they only *appear to be* vulnerable. That is the result of a Twelve-Step spiritual program in action.

By the Grace of God, and with the help of others in this great fellowship, I don't have to hide my feelings any longer. I can now communicate with my loved ones and other members and reveal my Spirit, which was in hiding before working the Twelve Steps. I become exceptionally vulnerable when I do that, but today that's okay. It is only by being vulnerable that I found my true love of a lifetime; far better late than never.

# PART IV
## The Maintenance Steps—

## Ten, Eleven, and Twelve

# 38

## *My Spiritual Journey Changed How I Perceived Reality*

**Step Ten: Continued to take personal inventory and when we were wrong promptly admitted it.**

I think we each have a unique spirituality we've been blessed with by working the Twelve Steps. I can explain what spirituality means to me, but it may be quite different for you. I like to think that my own spirituality is reflected each twenty-four hours in my Step Ten inventory by asking myself: "How do I show love and respond to others?" "How do I take care of my own feeling of well-being?" "Do I let others see my genuine heart and soul, or am I still hiding at times behind a false front?" "Do I take time to help newcomers and carefully listen to their feelings?"

Doing a daily Step Ten inventory makes me aware of emotions and needs that motivated me to act in unhealthy ways in the past, and some of them still can, if I don't stay connected to a Higher Power. Although I sometimes hate to admit it, self-exploration has helped me realize that because I was so stuck in self-pity in that active alcoholic marriage, I wanted someone to sympathize and assure me that I had the right to feel sorry for myself. I had become a martyr and victim that needed validation from others. There were, of course, other times when anger, resentments, or need for control were my motivating forces.

I love this saying by the famous "Anonymous," "Thinking is when my mouth is closed and my head keeps talking to itself." I spend most of my days in social interactions, speaking or being spoken to, and it's important to take time to communicate with my own Spirit. I need quality time each day to spend alone to keep in touch with who I am and where I'm headed, with the help of my God. If I want to experience serenity, I need that special sacred time to be with Him and let Him love me, so that I may develop an understanding of His wisdom. Serenity allows me to have a porous quality of heart and soul wherein all good things from God can enter and remain. I believe that is the purpose of our Tenth Step inventory.

I feel God's protection against most evil things today, but I never really thought much about angels before working the program. I believe they do exist and they have a purpose, according to God's plan for them, as He does for me. For some reason, previous to Al-Anon, I never thought about them being used by Him to guard me.

As a child, I loved the name Timothy, and when I became an adult, I was interested in the Biblical stories about St. Timothy. I seemed to be mystically drawn to him. I think maybe it was because he was a physically weak person (as I myself tend to be), but he was written in the scriptures as being very sweet and spiritual. When I converted to my chosen faith about fifteen years ago, I was Divinely guided to look to St. Timothy to be my guardian angel. I like to think of him now as giving God reminders—in a loving way—about where I am and the direction he (St. Timothy) thinks I should be heading. In the beginning of my Twelve-Step journey, believing that St. Timothy was looking out for me made it much easier to let go of my problems and confidently let God be in charge. You might want to think about inviting an angel into your life, if you haven't already done so.

Before finding a Twelve-Step program, my understanding of spirituality was religious and attending traditional church services. I really had no concept of the reality and power of spirituality, as we know it in our fellowship. As I look back, I can easily see why my life was empty and incomplete for so long. I was always incessantly questioning and searching for answers to fill the void I felt inside.

I've belonged to an organized religion and church and have had a strong belief in God most of my life. I "believed" in Him, but it never really occurred to me to trust Him enough to turn my whole life entirely over to His complete care, and thus free myself of anxieties. When I was able to do so, I found a spiritual connection that brought me a great sense of peace and acceptance. I thought I knew all I had to know about God, yet the people I found in my support group were genuinely happy, and I was not. I was convinced I had to have what they had, so they told me to keep coming back until I *wanted* to keep coming back.

I grew up with a Christian prayer which in part states, "Thy will be done," but I only gave those words lip service. They really didn't govern my life at that time, because everything had to be "My-way-be-done." But I do desire that His will be done now, and only He knows His big plan for me. Looking back, I can see that He's always had His arms around me, leading and guiding me. I am just now becoming more aware of that, with the help of the program. I spent a lifetime not facing reality, and that type of thinking is not unlearned overnight.

I think part of my spirituality evolved when I first I came to believe that God was all around me because of my love of nature as a child, and I still find Him there. Then I came to believe that God lives within me in my soul and that is His domain. Finally, in my senior years, I came to believe that God is everything and there is nothing else; I am absolutely nothing without Him. That happened when I came to believe that God is simply love.

It took a long time working the Steps before I could trust God to be in charge and just let things happen, but today I can. The way God is working in my life is great. As a result, I have learned to just let it happen as it is. My lessons came in many ways. In the beginning, I really had to struggle with what I heard in the meetings and in the literature. I was still in denial of my part in the active alcoholic marriage, and I was very frustrated and confused about what I was reading, hearing about the program, and working the Steps. All I could focus on was my pain, self-pity, and feelings of hopelessness and helplessness.

I didn't realize it at that time, but slowly and very subtly, everything I was hearing was being filed away in my subconscious mind for later use. As time went by, working the program, I realized that I was finding an answer within me for most of the lessons my Higher Power was offering me, because He just keeps repeating His life's lessons until I pull up the answer that is right for me. I've also discovered that it's not a matter of "take what you like and leave the rest," as some of us quote in meetings. Slowly but surely, I find solutions from insights stored in my subconscious that others have shared in meetings during stressful situations they have experienced.

Some of my lessons are painful; others are pure joy. I don't get to choose which ones come to me today. That's okay, because I get to choose how I work through them, with God's help. Out of some of my most painful times have come my greatest periods of growth. I was told one time to look for the gift; the lesson to be learned in hurtful situations. I believe now that God can use emotional pain as a recovery tool. Sometimes it comes as a result of my own stinking thinking, but whenever and wherever it happens, I can learn from it and move on with my life, and another lesson is completed.

I used to feel that if things were going really well for me, it was the lull between storms. (Talk about expectations…) Now I believe that I can keep my serenity during any storm, with the help of my Higher Power. I also believe now that a lot of the chaos in my first marriage was caused by my insanity, my reactions to the disease. I was so wrapped up in my own pain of coping with his disease that I didn't realize that someone (like my former alcoholic husband) who is hurting so badly him/her self, is probably not emotionally equipped to deal with my pain. The lesson I learned from that, the gift, is to have compassion for any alcoholic. Today I can accept a crisis as it comes; the difference now is that I don't have to *create one*. In some situations, I can use those thoughts to accept that someone is verbally attacking me because of their *own* emotional pain, and I can detach from it.

If something is troubling me, or if I think I maybe owe amends to someone, I can run it by my sober AA husband and we can talk about my feelings. If I need the understanding of a woman-to-woman point of view, I can go to my current sponsor or other long-time mentors in the program; however, I firmly believe that nothing is more helpful than writing about the things I'm discovering about myself. I have probably averaged a minimum of an hour a day doing that since I first began Al-Anon, and I'm convinced writing has contributed greatly to my healing.

Others in the fellowship taught me that every day you should reach out and touch someone—and not just literally; almost all others love a human touch: holding hands, a warm hug, a friendly kiss on the cheek. (If it's a newcomer, I ask them first if they need a hug.) People may forget what I say, people may forget what I do, but I'm sure *people will never forget how I made them feel.* Spiritual encounters are beyond all of my control and are never exactly what I *expect,* so I can just "Let Go and Let God" do His work.

As my thinking changes, so also will my true self, my values, attitudes, responses, and actions. I surrender the person that was carefully molded and formed by my past experiences, according to the values of others. I am like the butterfly, breaking loose from its own cocoon, and I'm finally free to be me.

When I work the Twelve Steps on a daily basis, especially my Tenth Step inventory, I reassure myself that I'll be able to overcome anything that has happened in the past and live a much more peaceful life today. As the steps change my way of acting and reacting, I am growing, and therefore, the atmosphere I create changes, and that is another miracle of the Twelve Steps.

# 39

## *Practicing True Humility*

Humility is essential for my spiritual security. I know I can't be my own doctor, attorney, electrician, etc., and I can get in trouble fast if I think I can; I need an expert. That forced me to turn to the God *of my understanding* for help in the Steps, and that was the beginning of my special relationship with Him.

I used to think of true humility as the example I've seen in videos on TV of some people crawling all the way to an alter in a Catholic Church as a penance for their sins; an act of surrender and contrition to God. I've always had a great reverence for the religious God *of my understanding*; however, He wasn't a living reality for me. Before finding my support groups, I didn't want anyone else, including God, *telling me what to do*. Working the Twelve Steps and the example of others in our program helps me recognize God at work in my life and that of others, and that is how I practice humility now.

I love old spiritual tales, and I think this one can be applied to Step Eleven in my program. "A scholar went to his mentor and asked him, "Teach me humility." The old wise man replied, "I cannot do that, because humility is a teacher in itself. It is learned by means of practice. If you cannot practice it, you cannot learn it." I humbly believe the "it" in that story is for me what Step Eleven is all about: practicing humility, but everything I've learned has taken me endless practice. In Step Three, the word "will" refers to our thoughts and feelings and our "lives" refers to our actions. When I pray, using Step Eleven, I am asking to know what thoughts and feelings God wants me to have, and I'm praying for the power to turn them into actions.

Humility led me out of isolation, and my Higher Power helped me get there through daily conscious contact with Him. In having the humility to surrender to God's will, I have to be willing to take risks; without putting limitations or boundaries on myself. It truly is a matter of "Let Go and Let God."

I believe that to have faith, there must be a continuing daily rebirth and activity of heart and mind toward understanding God. I can't do the program of Twelve Steps passively, because it's a program of action. (The word "step" indicates action.) Part of the action for me means I have to spend daily time with God by reading the Scriptures at random and praying that He will explain His Word to me. His Words have the power to motivate me and give me a sense of direction.

As my thinking change, my true values, attitudes, responses, and actions also change. Mainly because the Steps are a process of surrendering up to God the person I had become, based on others perspectives, and following their values; instead of listening to my own truths. I first had to find my own authentic being through the spirituality in the Twelve Steps, and with the help of a Higher Power, I have.

I had absolutely no clue what the word meditation in Step Eleven meant. I read a lot of books about it, and I learned to relax my body, but unfortunately, it did not include all of the chatter in my mind! I discovered that getting in conscious contact with God is not the same as filling my mind with new thoughts from spiritual reading, nor is it new knowledge gained by reading program literature. It's none of those things. My spiritual convictions today lead me to believe that it's having the humility to be still and receive guidance from the voice of the Spirit of God within.

# 40

# *Receiving and Practicing God's Wisdom in My Life by the Use of Step Eleven*

**Step Eleven: Sought through prayer and meditation to improve our conscious contact with God, *as we understood Him,* praying only for knowledge of His will for us and the power to carry it out.**

Other members taught me that I had to take time to *notice* the roses in my life before I'd be able to take the time to *smell them.* Being appreciative of the small wonders that a Higher Power puts before me is one of the blessings of having inner peace in any given moment now. To my mind, the fragrance of a rose is mystic, in the same way I think of spirituality. I cannot possess it the way I do material things; I can only treasure it in my senses. I think somewhere in the Bible it states: "Where your heart is, also will your treasure be." Living life to the fullest extent I possibly can means going spiritually inward to find answers to any challenges put before me.

In the beginning, a mentor explained this to me: "Do you want to stubbornly keep holding life in your own hands, Mary, or are you willing to let God have it and manage it? Do you want to keep using God for what you want to do, or are you willing to become teachable and let Him use you?" Listening to God's voice now means: receiving His guidance one day following another, and at times one moment after another.

I didn't like the expression Higher Power when I first heard it in meetings. It almost seemed sacrilegious to me, especially the idea that a Higher Power could be anything I chose; why, even a doorknob! Somehow I couldn't imagine my Power Greater as a doorknob. Then I reached the Third Step and became aware of the words, "God *as we understood Him.*" I liked that statement because others in the program are imperfect human beings—as I am—with no better, or less, understanding of the spirituality of our program. What fits them does not necessarily mean it has to fit me.

Knowing that God *as I understand Him* meant that I could let my Spirit grow, evolve, and change, at my *own* speed, made all of the difference in the world to me as to how I worked the Steps of the program. This is one of the things I love about being in my Twelve-Step family groups: I don't have to defend my beliefs. I grew up in a country where there's a lot of bigotry and everyone is still at war about religion. Thinking of that still makes me feel sad.

I'm a recovering perfectionist, and I had to keep busy making everything "just so." Now I can give myself permission to slow down, even do absolutely nothing but meditate; take time out and space just for Mary-Glen. Doing that process was much too painful before Al-Anon, for the simple reason it encouraged me to concentrate on self-pity and feelings of victimization. Taking precious time for myself now is helping me recover from a lifetime of emotional hurts.

All of my life, I harbored feelings of abandonment and rejection by those closest to me. I longed for someone to be really loving and caring to me. Even some of the members of my chosen church had somewhat ostracized me after my divorce because they felt, "How could she leave that poor man after all of those years?" (One of them was happy to rush that gossip to me.) Only a longtime survivor of living with the active disease knows the answer to that one and can give me the love and support I am looking for. We only find that in a Twelve-Step fellowship. I will add that the Pastor of my church supported my decision to leave an actively drinking alcoholic that refused to seek sobriety and chose to continue on a path of destruction. He felt I should be nominated for Sainthood by having put up with it for a lifetime.

In one of my first meetings, I remember a lady sharing about her relationship with a loving Higher Power. I felt sadness overwhelming me, but it wasn't the same emotions like listening to a sad song or a sad movie. I believe the tears were an expression of the deepest part of my soul in yearning to have that type of relationship with my religious God. But how could I have that relationship with Him when I had so many committees in my head ruling my actions and insane behavior? Those were a good example of self-will run riot, just as the active alcoholics experience.

Before working the program, I used to make plans and decisions, then as an afterthought, I'd pray for God's blessings and ask for His help in the process of doing them! When I did that, I would end up (of course) feeling that my prayers were not being answered. The solution was, I had to take a special time every single day to meditate and try to have a two-way prayer time with my God. My prayers before Al-Anon were a one-way dialogue with a headstrong chairperson in my head doing all of the talking. My wisdom was coming from my own self-will, and that was like the *blind leading the blind.* I was never a good listener, so I had to learn to practice listening. It took endless enthusiastic practice, as it had done when I learned to swim as a child, ride a bicycle, and play piano as an adult.

My attempts to have conscious contact with my religious God led me to believe that I should not limit myself to filling my mind with spiritual thoughts from reading or from others sharing their thoughts with me. I tried to receive guidance and new insights from an *entirely new source*; regretfully, that was an unfamiliar voice to me at that time: *The Spirit of a Power Greater Than Myself, whom I've always called "God."*

It took a lot of time and effort to get to the point where I could develop a communication with God and really let go of all people, places, and situations. It also meant finding true humility, which has taken me many years in the program. But the rewards of all of this are well worth it, since I've been given the gift of a spiritual source of wisdom, which touches my life and also benefits my loved ones in a special way. I try to pass on to others the wisdom I receive, not only by sponsorship, but also in my writing, which I share with others. A spiritual mentor told me, "Writing is the soul made visible, and to keep what I've been given I have to pass it on to others." Our program tells us, "Until we give up believing that we can handle our lives completely by ourselves, we never will seek God's help. He will never butt in where He's not wanted. He waits for us to call on Him."

Listening to my inner voice took lots of practice and courage. I find that change doesn't happen overnight. I have to do something over and over before I own it, until it just becomes second nature. I needed courage to be willing to step out into the unknown; to be willing to take action on the messages my inner voice was giving me. I had to practice distinguishing between God's voice (my inner voice) and the other voices in my head that wanted to lead me away from my Higher Power. It was difficult, but that is what leads us to "Let Go and Let God." I like the image of God as the Good Shepherd, and the saying, "Only His sheep know His voice." I listen to His special voice now, and that helps to avoid allowing my feelings to lead me astray.

God has always spoken to me in my thoughts and my own language. I have had the spiritual experience, when my life was in extreme danger because of alcoholism, of hearing myself speak in tongues. But normally my prayers to and from God are in my own language of English; with a slight Scottish accent, of course! That's how He gets my attention; through my practicing the art of listening.

Sometimes, even now, my fears, feelings of helplessness, old behavior and thinking patterns can take over and block me from hearing His voice. Even after years of lots of two-way prayer, sometimes all I hear is the incessant chatter of my own self-thoughts running amok. If I only pray to God and never take the time to listen that becomes just a "monologue" with Mary-Glen doing all of the talking, because I am sure God is too wise to interrupt me in that type of endeavor. After all, He does let me learn from my mistakes. I won't make too much progress in growth in the program in that way, nor will I help anyone else along the way. Besides which, when the old committees in my head are in charge, how can I possibly hear the voice of God?

The principles of Step Eleven have evolved for me as follows: God Speaks; God has a plan for my life; And God will reveal that plan in His time—not "Mary-my-way's" if I am open and willing enough to listen and follow His directions.

I believe God gave me intelligence, judgment, and the power to carry those out. He also gives me free will to use those, as I choose. Being given that awareness was indeed a spiritual awakening for me. When I turned my life and will over to His care in Step Three, it became easier to make the correct choices, because He guides me with His wisdom. But I had to learn to listen before I could hear God's voice, which has taken me many years of concentration. He has a compassionate voice, compared to the unruly voices in charge of my head for so long. Many times His voice helps me feel comfortable with a decision I've reached or a certain course of action I may be planning to take. Now and again, I discover that He may be telling me to be very cautious about trusting an individual or a situation.

It used to be that trusting in God's voice felt as if I were lost in a maze of pathways, mirrors, hallways, doors, and there were choices I could make that would lead me to many dead ends. (As a teenager I can remember on a date we would have fun at the carnivals going through mazes set up like that. I think they called them the "crazy houses" in those days.) Following God's direction is a little easier now. It's like walking down a dark hallway and He lets a little light shine through under each door. If I follow that light, I can open those doors one at a time and receive the gifts behind each one, such as faith, unconditional love, strength, encouragement, and hope. Following a Greater Power's guidance has become a better path for me to walk in my daily life, because He is always there as my companion.

Writing that paragraph reminds me of an experience I had as a child of about eight years old. My little wirehaired dog Pal hated being confined to a leash, but that day I had to walk him through the main part of the village and he had to be leashed. I had a vivid imagination, and I decided to play "blind man being led by a dog." I would be the "blind man" being led by Pal on his leash. There were huge, old-fashioned light standards with deep ridges of metal all the way up them on the village Main Street. I decided about that point in our walk to close my eyes and let Pal "guide" me. Well, being a male dog, he headed straight for one of those poles, dragging me unsuspectingly behind him, and I woke up on the ground with blood streaming from my forehead. A lady saw me and took me into her home to give me first aid. I still have that deep scar on my forehead; one of many I'm afraid that were left untreated by medical care when I was a child.

The lesson from recalling that story is this: If I pray daily for God's guidance and listen for His voice, *I will be led in the proper direction.* He knows what is best for me. I can't see sometimes where I'm being led and what's ahead of me, but *He does,* because He's already there, and I can trust Him completely.

I once heard a speaker describe hearing the quietness of serenity as the "gentle hum of the stars and the quiet heartbeat of the world." (Author anonymous). Loving natural surroundings as I do, I can appreciate that saying. During the time when I was living with the actively drinking alcoholic, I always had a deep longing to live way out in the middle of the countryside somewhere—miles and miles from anywhere. I thought peace and contentment would be mine if I could only hear the songs of the wild birds and other beautiful sounds of nature—and not much else! In retrospect, I don't think I actually wanted to be a hermit, for I do love people; rather, I think I was just afraid of life itself. Today, I know I can't live without others in our programs that are using the Twelve Steps way of life. They helped me find serenity, and they continue helping me keep it. I no longer have any desire to live in isolation.

Even after a year or so of working the Steps, I would use self-will run riot and always be in perpetual motion—take off in many directions at once—and all before my brain had time to get *into gear.* When I had no direction and my thinking was fragmented, old distorted anxieties and fear would take over, causing me to forget about self-care. Pretty soon I'd be chasing one unrealistic dream or another, looking for someone/something else to make me feel "all better" again. I'd end up feeling like a completely lost child with no one to guide me.

Today, I may be involved in many interests and service activities, but I handle only one at a time, one direction at a time, and one day at a time. I think a focused program person will usually hear one voice more strongly than the others, and follow that one. I can see now that for a long time I had stuffed so much garbage into my Spirit from obsessing about an actively drinking alcoholic that it probably became almost impossible for God to reach me.

I always thought I had to be busy 24/7, so I never took the special time out to sit down and get away from it all; have some quiet space around me. (I also make sure now there's no phone in the room to which I retreat.) I now believe I am deserving and worthy enough to have a special time and space, and I continue to pray for the ability to communicate with God.

Following His will today means understanding that although I can make plans, I do not predict the outcome. I take whatever action I need to take and leave the rest up to God. Before I had accepted that belief, it was proven to me so many times that the things, persons, or results I had begged to receive would have been harmful for me if my prayers had been answered. Today I can simply pray, "God, I'm going to try to do, such and such a thing; however, I am quick to add, "But thy will be done. Please help me accept that, and guide me."

I find there are still many situations where I have to carefully use the tools of the program in order to keep my peace. I need to repeat Slogans and take any Steps or actions the program has given me, which will lead to peaceful, harmonious, solutions; to keep my focus on what is in my control, and let go of what is not. It is becoming easier because of Step Eleven to be part of the solution instead of part of the problem, and I experience more and more during tough times that I can keep that peaceful feeling, no matter what happens.

I try to stay focused on my inner spirit. Some others see being focused on oneself as pursuing dreams and goals, some call it "knowing what your true purpose in life is," some look at all of that as keeping centered. I understand it as simply making sure that I keep God as the center of my life and my main focus. Everything else falls into place where it's supposed to be, if I follow that priority.

It's my personal belief that I am a spiritual being who is having a human experience in this lifetime, and that God installed my spirit before I was born. It has been growing and evolving ever since, and working the Twelve Steps of the program has helped this process immensely. A lifetime of religious teachings taught me the theory and history of God's love, but each and every one in my program has helped me *experience it.* I've also come to believe, by working the steps, that all I had to do all along was simply have faith in God as I did when I was a child;

that is, in an inquisitive, open, sensitive, trusting way. That Higher-Powered insight is a true blessing for me; something I can forever use to better my life.

The spirituality, wisdom, and improved personality I have today are all gifts from God. I can't earn them, win them, scale a mountain, beg or bargain for these gifts of the program; a Power Greater Than Myself freely gives them to me. He only expects gratitude from me in return. When I am thankful for all of my blessings I am showing love, respect and obedience to His will, and I am granted inner peace. I then become more able to see the reality of that Power working in my life and the lives of others. It all began with prayer and meditation, and I make sure now that my special prayer time begins with praise and thanks for all that He has blessed me with.

If you are considering joining a Twelve-Step program, I'm sure you will find hope with an understanding of the Steps that you can have peace and harmony in a permanent way in your life. We have had many, many miracles in the groups. It took lots of Step Three and Step Eleven for me, and it's my humble opinion we can do Step Eleven (sought through prayer and meditation) even as a newcomer. We work the Steps in order, one at a time with a sponsor; nevertheless, if we believe as in Step One that we're powerless, what are we supposed to do with that feeling of powerlessness? I'm confident it's acceptance and surrender to a Power Greater, because prayer and meditation are an intimate spiritual conversation with Him.

I learned to devote a certain amount of time every morning to reading our Twelve-Step literature, meditate, and pray for guidance "Just for today." There are many times when I read my daily program meditation books and my mind will sometimes wander, or I tell myself, "This one doesn't apply to me right now." But if I ask God first to tell me what He wants me to hear, before I start reading them, then I can concentrate on what is written in front of me. If I say that prayer first, I make myself more open to receiving His message from the reading and apply it to my life that particular day.

The program has taught me to develop a relationship with the God *of my understanding* that is uniquely my own—not necessarily one that's influenced by other's beliefs, but rather on the voice of my own inner self. Some others call that voice my "intuition" or that "gut feeling." I prefer to think of it as the core of my heart and the depths of my soul.

Surrender to the greater power of God means that my life is under new management, and I do not control the flow of life as He sends it around me. I've learned to relax and just let myself simply "be." Before doing the program process of acceptance and surrender, especially the first three Steps, I saw the world as a hostile, frightening place in which I was doomed to exist. Today I know that was a prison of my own making. I can't blame my actively drinking former husband; I had condemned and sentenced myself to be there.

When I came to the recovery rooms, in order to experience tranquility I stopped reading the newspapers and watching the news on TV. I was convinced it was the only way, at that time anyway, that I could feel a Divine Presence, whom I already knew as God, was available to me; therefore, I surrendered all of the violence in the world news to Him. I had a great fear that my first husband would kill me with his gun since I had finally left him forever, and there were a few instances of that type of shooting of younger women in Las Vegas at that time. Once I abandoned my self-will to God, I was able to view the world differently, and I began to experience what serenity could mean to me.

My world now means the people I come in contact with; today, tonight, tomorrow, and the next day. The people God provides to love and comfort me *are my world now.* With the help of Step Ten, I have to ask myself daily, "What sort of spiritual atmosphere am I creating in my world around me, and how am I affecting the reality in which I am now living?" As we say in the program: "Sometimes my actions speak so loudly others can't hear a darn thing I am saying!" People need to see the *results* of my changes by working the Twelve-Step principles; listening to God's guidance is helping me do that.

The spirituality process of working the Steps has led me to believe that God does have a plan—a blueprint, so to speak—of my life that is far superior to anything I could ever have dreamed up. It's a plan that guarantees that I'll have the serenity I always longed for, but could never experience. I don't need to know the details of God's plan for my future, or even a year ahead; I only need to be guided one day at a time.

I never knew or believed that way before coming to these rooms. God was the "Big Boss" of the universe, but an inferiority complex led me to feel I was too insignificant to be recognized by Him as a worthwhile human being. As an adult, I was always questioning and analyzing the big mystery of life. It was a case of, "show me proof, Lord, and I'll believe." I am now convinced that I don't have to question or analyze God, *as I understand Him*; I only have to accept Him with my heart and soul.

I love to look up at the mountains where I now live in this beautiful desert valley that God created at some point in time. I used to feel so insignificant compared to them, but now that I truly love myself, I can accept that I am a special part of His plan for the universe. I might be just a wee sparkle on this planet, but

I am confident that God does know who I am and where I am today. I'm learning to love and appreciate my own uniqueness, one special moment at a time.

When I began working the program, I had to learn to verbalize and communicate my feelings to others. I had stuffed them most of my life, and I really didn't know where to begin. My sponsor told me to write down what I was feeling (or thought I was), and what I thought I could do about it for my own emotional and spiritual health. Then, I'd call her, read it to her, and we'd talk about it. I began to carry 3 x 5 index cards with me at all times, and I'd write down whatever thoughts I wanted to save to share with her. That was my first attempts at communication, *trust in another human being, and unconditional love with God's help.* It was also the beginning of a passion for writing about my spirituality that continues to grow today. It has made an enormous contribution to my healing and growth in the program.

In my early years of the program, before I'd go to sleep I'd pray, "I have this problem (whatever it might be) and I need a solution." A program mentor taught me: "Mary, God's going to be up all night anyway, so why not give it to Him?" I'd wake up in the middle of the night and hear this "voice" telling me a great way to take care of the problem I would never have came up with. I knew it must be my Power Greater, because there was no one else in my home at that time, and the solution was so far away from what the committees in the head had drafted out for me!

Today, I often find that if God is carrying me along toward any new dreams and goals, whatever I am excited and passionate about, He will communicate what my next steps should be. He can still do that in the middle of the night. I sometimes wonder if He thinks that is the only time He can get my full attention? So I keep a pad and pen on my nightstand—just in case—and that way I don't forget the message by the time morning comes.

Occasionally, if I forget to pray first and start thinking about an exciting project I am planning for today or the near future, suddenly I might hear the gentle inner voice of my P.G. say, "Did you forget about me?" Or "Where do I fit into your plans?" Or "Are you trying to take over my job again?" Or even more jolting, "Oh no! You're doing that again!" It is then that I am reminded to always pray to Him *first* for guidance; even if I have to do that many times in one day. When I'm sewing and I botch it, it's because I forgot even one more time.

I'm convinced that the principle of praying for guidance and protection from a Higher Power is the main root of the Twelve-Step program, and also the principle we have of loving and supporting one another. How do I receive that guidance? Well, Gabrielle doesn't come in with his horn and suddenly have God exclaim, "Here I am with the answers for you!" Rather, the answers come as subtle awakenings and whispers from my quiet voice within.

I had to learn to listen to God, to separate my self-will thoughts from His thoughts. It was difficult for me to accept the concept that I could get directly in touch with the God *of my understanding* by asking questions in my prayers, and that He would answer me by giving me guidance and directions. It all seemed so far out (no pun intended); however, the beliefs of some emotionally healthy program people led me to believe that *I could also do that.* It became obvious to me that they had been given a faith and power in living I had never experienced myself. I decided to follow in their footsteps, and I have found a beautiful new way of living and confidence in a Higher Power.

I have no coincidences in my life today; I know it's my Power Greater at work (like the Aha! moments when the light bulb flashes). What I used to think of as *intuition,* or a *great idea,* I gradually accepted to be the quiet peaceful voice of God speaking to me. My self-will speaks in a loud, demanding harsh language. I can tell that committee today, "I don't need you; be quiet."

I believe that others and I receive guidance from a Higher Power in whatever manner feels comfortable, as long as it's actually my own inner voice I'm hearing/ listening to, and not the results of someone else's thinking; for example: astrology Charts, tarot cards, ouija boards, self-proclaimed psychics, or reading tea leaves. (My mother was great at that last one in Scotland. She had quite a following of young women who really believed the make-believe she told them.) My humble opinion about fortune-telling guidance is that it may be fun, but I feel it is merely illusions or fantasies coming from someone else's mind and perceptions. I am open to suggestions from others who are putting a lot of time and effort into working their program, but my guidance *has to be from my own* Power Greater Than Myself. As we say in my Twelve-Step program: "Take what you like in what I'm sharing and leave the rest!"

I never use an alarm clock. I just seem to awaken about the same time each morning, and when I get up I tell Him, "Thank you, God, for waking me up and giving me the gift of another beautiful new twenty-four hours." That prayer is especially important for me, because when I worked for the School District we had two young people die in their sleep. One had been celebrating a wedding anniversary with her husband in Las Vegas, and he woke up the next morning to find her dead. The other was a young custodian who also died in somewhat similar circumstances. Remembering them keeps me in the present day only.

My second prayer in the morning is gratitude for my good physical and emotional health, and then I ask Him to guide me in every single thing I do or say today. Sometimes I repeat that prayer many times a day. Then I get my coffee, make myself comfortable, and quietly give my deepest feelings to God. I may not hear Him every single morning; however, when I am able to hear Him respond, I write down exactly what I hear, because I believe now that is His ways of helping me understand myself and grow. I use large index cards for my writing, and I usually don't daily journal as such. I write when the Spirit moves me.

The words can come very quickly to me in those special moments with Him, but they can disappear even more quickly if I don't grasp them for myself in writing and forever keep them close to my soul. I've been told that I should write down whatever and whenever the words of His guidance come to me without going back to change any of it. If I should go back and rewrite something I believe comes from my Power Greater, I am once again going back into old behavior of letting "Mary-my-will-be-done." I'm convinced now that He's leading and guiding me, so I have no dread today of any gossip, criticism, or condemnation of anything I say or do now. I can share my thoughts, verbally or in writing, and express how I feel in truth and love; with no trepidation at all.

I live a very contented, serene life today. With daily prayer and meditation, God provides the wisdom, the tools, and a Power that never fails, and the rest is up to me. I find, in my recovery from living with the disease of alcoholism, that no path is the best path or the only path. Only my Higher Power knows the proper direction for me at any given time.

I'm quite sure some of you are probably wondering at this point about the big "Million dollar question:" How do I know when it's God's voice speaking to me and not my own self-will, that old self-appointed Higher Power of mine? Good question, but I think an easy-to-answer one after years of practice.

God's voice makes me feel tranquil. He speaks to me in a compassionate, loving way. If I am being guided to make a major change in my life in some way and it comes from the deepest part of my soul, I know it is from Him. I feel safe, a feeling of respite, a secure feeling of *letting go*, and that everything will indeed be okay.

I have to confess there are times it's a little scary following God's guidance, since I often don't know where I'm being led. I compare that to being back around the ocean in the heavy fog in Orange County (and especially in Glasgow, Scotland), where I could only see a few steps ahead of me if I were walking, or a few feet while driving. But as we say in our fellowship: "I have to trust that if I keep putting one foot in front of the other, eventually I'll be led to the place I hope to be; and I am supposed to be." And it has been working that way for me.

When I became receptive to God's voice, He offered me His prescription for tranquility. He gives me a sense of clarity and direction, and He's helping me follow my dreams and goals. I'm confident He'll never take me where I don't belong, and I am becoming very serene and happy following His gentle voice. My soul is calling out for "more, more" of that good "stuff." Before, I was always searching for that "more, more," however, I do know where to find it now.

If you have never practiced writing down your thoughts in daily meditation time, you may be wondering if this will all really work in your life. Well, here's the way I see it: Through ancient and modern times in history, many famous spiritual people have been convinced in faith that they are recording mystically what they believe to be the words from a Higher Power's voice. They have passed it on from one generation to another in the Holy Bible, the scriptures, and reading their beliefs has strengthened my own belief in my Power Greater, whom I've always known as God.

I believe our Twelve-Step programs also work in that manner. The founders of both of our programs firmly believed that God would give them all of the answers they ever needed, and they did indeed receive their answers, and a miracle, when it all came to pass. What they have written has been passed on to others in both programs, and now on to me. To receive that wisdom I only have to keep an inquisitive, open, willing, accepting mind, and use the principles in all of my relationships on a daily basis. It absolutely works—if we work it—not just when we think about it. Now, if all of this worked to benefit and improve other's lives that have gone before me, I'm confident it will also work for me. It has—and it still does.

Asking for knowledge of God's will for me, and the power to carry it out, is a prayer to which I will always receive a positive answer. It's obvious to me now that listening to God's voice is rather like the effects of the wind. I can see and hear the effects of the wind blowing by the increasing activity of the branches on the trees and the rustling of the leaves, but I can't actually see the wind itself. In the same light, there is no way I can prove to anyone that I am receiving guidance from the voice of a Power Greater Than Myself. Nevertheless, I hope others will be able to see the effects of my following His wisdom and will—by my actions and my behavior—just like the wind.

# 41

## *My Personal Gifts of the Program and Thoughts about Step Twelve*

**Step Twelve: Having had a spiritual awakening as a result of these steps, we tried to carry this message to others, and to practice these principles in all our affairs.**

In trying to carry the message to others who need it, I pray that my speech and attitudes will show evidence that my life was transformed by working the Twelve Steps. Not by using a false image as I did previously in my battle with the disease, but just by honestly being myself. In other words, I want my behavior and thinking to reflect who I am inwardly and what I'm all about after working a Twelve-Step program for a number of years. By doing this, I may help others find hope and faith that the program will also work for them, just by sharing my experiences with them. When I am busy helping others, I know I don't ever have to go very far to find my God, for He's already there.

My Twelve-Step program has many gifts just for my taking, but no one can get them for me. Recently a friend shared these thoughts with me: "God gives every bird its food, but He doesn't throw it into their nest!" That means I have footwork that has to be done, however, I stay out of planning the results, or as some call it "the outcome."

The serenity I own today is the result of many dedicated members of our Twelve-Step program who have walked the path before me and shared their solutions with me of what worked best for them. They are an unending spiritual source that I can draw on, and if what I am sharing now will help even one person, then I will also move another step forward. I can only keep what I've been blessed with by giving it away.

Someone shared recently about the problem of having envy, and they added that envy is a hostile self-pity. I can genuinely say that I have no envy in my heart today of anyone's possessions or achievements; I'm happy for them. Envy would only lead me to be discontented and ungrateful for the things I now own, and those are my gifts of the program and my God. Those gifts give me serenity.

I could never find true and lasting serenity in relationships by accumulating money and/or material possessions, nor by escaping reality, using alcohol, or fantasy ways of thinking. Those things are all of my own mind and self-will. I feel emphatically that for Mary-Glen, serenity is an "inside job." I had to change my attitudes and reactions to the outside world. Now I believe that my world ends at the International Airport near our home. That thought alone is a gift that keeps me serene—one day at a time.

I think the knowledge we gain in the process of a Twelve-Step program is empowering. I'm an avid reader, and I believe words have a special power to inspire, motivate, and change me, if I allow that to happen. As I absorb the information in our Al-Anon literature, and some outside spiritual material, the stronger becomes my power over old feelings and behavior.

Spending so many hours studying the Twelve Steps in my recovery may not pay off for me in dollars, but the main benefit is that it does make life much more complete and interesting. I'm learning on my journey to never let one road end without finding another, guided, of course, by God's directions. He is my guide, with an awesome map, and I want to keep looking for new challenges and working on self-discovery, regardless of how old I am.

I plan to use the Twelve Steps and God's wisdom in my daily actions to find new and exciting things to do for the rest of whatever time I have left on this earth, and what is most important of all, to help others discover within them what I've been given. That is what carrying the message means. I believe that I am now one of our program miracles. I was given a victory over the disease that is cunning, baffling, and tries to destroy all that it possibly can.

Today I have complete trust that God will provide for all of my needs and that all of my challenges will be worked out. I deeply care for all others, but I have learned not to care about what they think about me. It's interesting to think of it that way now, though, because when I started not caring about what people thought of me, I began to get lots of messages that they think I'm wonderful! And I am able to return that admiration and unconditional love back to them.

No one now has the power to control my thinking and actions; in fact, since working and practicing the principles of the Twelve Steps, no one has the power to upset me in any way at all. Self-exploration and many spiritual awakenings along the way led me to feel this way and have no fear, because God is always walking ahead of me; wherever I may go.

Perhaps having a difficult childhood led me to develop a great need to search for spirituality in my life; therefore, I have learned with God's help to benefit from it all. He is gradually sending special people into my life; when the time is right we come together by His Divine appointment. I share my feelings and solutions with them, and that helps them find their own answers that are buried within themselves, as mine were for a long time. It's such a great warm feeling to help someone discover his/her own true self as I have.

When I feel God's presence and care, I have no dread of the future. It's in His hands. I had carried heavy burdens for so long which I felt would never end. At last I can feel excited and grateful for each day before me that God awakens and blesses me with.

A few years ago, God must have felt that I had recovered enough to be in a successful relationship with another man. I was beginning to long for a close companion, and feeling a little lonely. Unexpectedly, He sent my beloved Paul into my life who gives me all of the love, respect, care, and understanding I felt I previously lacked. We are in love with each other and have a strong commitment to help each other *become the best we can be*. He has twenty-five years of sobriety in AA, and we have a beautiful relationship because he is dedicated to working his program and passing it on to others, and we both work my very special Al-Anon program. God brought us together in His own mysterious way and we were happy to simply accept that gift from Him. We call how we met a "God thing." My Twelve-Step Family taught me that my happiness only begins with me, but having Paul in my life makes my joy complete.

I have many miles yet to travel and many lessons still to walk through and learn from, but the Twelve Steps have led me to a new life with a lot less emotional pain and a greater feeling of spiritual security. That is what serenity means for me today: what I have been *searching for all of my life*. Yes, this program works when you work it! When I used to think of Him as way out in space in the Universe somewhere above me, He seemed so out of reach for me to recognize and be aware of. Now that I think of Him as every loving act I do for you and you do for me, He has become *a living God*.

In other words, I don't want to think of my Power Greater Than Myself as only another philosophy of my program; I want to live His reality. Today I do that, with all of the love and support of others. When I look in their eyes, I see my God, and I hope they will see theirs in mine. To hang on to my spirituality I have to share it, give it away. The Scriptures tell us, "We reap what we sow." I reap much love today from all of the people in our Twelve-Step programs, and I am sure that is a source that has no ending. Their love is like "seed that fell on fertile ground" (also a quote from the scriptures), and I can see that love multiplying wherever I happen to be in my A.A. or Al-Anon family groups worldwide.

I like to think that I am a living example now; it's never too late to change and begin life anew. I hope and pray that I can be a reflection of all that is great and worthy in our Twelve-Step fellowship. By the simple clarity of whom I am and what I am all about, that I—and all other members like me—may attract and inspire others to try the Twelve-Step way of being transformed.

# PART V

*Where I Am Today*

# 42

## *Inner Peace and Complete Contentment*

I am living out the last chapters of my life with my beloved, sober A.A. husband, and I have never been more happy and serene. When I got over my phobia about flying by trusting in God, He opened up many doors for both of us. A few years ago, I finally went back home to Scotland and Ireland with Paul for the first time in over fifty years. I visited the little cottage in Millhall where I had been so spiritually happy as a child, and it looked just as I had remembered; with perhaps a few minor changes. I looked at the window that overlooked the dam in the little cottage where I used to sit, dream, and draw as a child, and it brought back many memories. I'm positive angels must have been my companions then.

We both love the gorgeous scenery and the loving, gracious Scottish people. They went out of their way to help us, and we sincerely appreciated that. Sadly to say, in our extremely busy city we don't see that type of brotherly love in action toward strangers very often. We'd love to live in Scotland, but we both feel we couldn't survive the climate. (Too much rain and cold.) Besides which, the real property in Scotland is becoming very expensive, almost as bad as California. We plan to return there soon for about a month or so and rent a "wee hoos" (Scottish dialect) so that we can fully experience it all. I'll probably start sounding like them all, but then Paul would like me to do that.

When we are among my relatives in Stirling, I have to interpret what they are saying sometimes, for Paul's benefit. Yes, they do speak the English language, but some of it is a Scottish dialect; and the MacGregor Clan and their friends speak so quickly, sometimes it's difficult to keep up with them. But we adore them all and they have much love, laughter, and spirituality in their lives. On many occasions we have gone to conventions of our fellowship in Oahu and Maui. We love Hawaii, but we couldn't afford to buy even a small house there, either. Paul's program sponsor lets us housesit for him on Maui when he comes over here to the mainland. I find that the Hawaiian Islands have an extremely spiritual atmosphere, wherever I am. While there one summer, I wrote a special chapter for this proposed book, for the simple reason my inner Spirit had no problem finding my mind receptive to whatever God wanted me to hear.

The more we participate in our fellowship conventions, the more friends we make, and that is the best part of it all. I had my first awakening to the fact that we are a worldwide spiritual fellowship when Paul and I attended the big International Convention in Minneapolis for five days a few years ago. There were approximately 65,000 people attending the opening ceremony in the large sports stadium. Even the entire floor of the stadium was packed with folding chairs that had been set up to accommodate the overflow, plus spaces for people in wheel chairs. All of the convention was extremely well organized, and it was a great joy to be part of it all. We were told that there were about 139 countries in the world now with meetings of the programs, and there were 89 countries represented in the opening ceremonies. (Some of the smaller countries I'd even forgotten existed.)

I was spiritually moved to tears when representatives from each country came out on the stage in their native costume. After they were announced, they presented their native flag, and they then gathered in a huge semi-circle around the bottom of the stage. It was very heart-warming for me, in particular, to see them all gathered in unconditional love, for the reason that I grew up in World War II when it seemed like the whole world was at war and people were being killed, even little children. To be together in that stadium with people from all over the world in unconditional love, peace, and harmony was very emotionally beautiful for me.

While there, we went to the online family marathon meetings and I was able to meet a few people that I had become friends with in an online committee. It always amazes me that people from all over the world can share our program on the computer; especially at the same time. I even met a group of Scottish people the first day we were at the main convention center who were all dressed in their kilt outfits and they were from my hometown of Glasgow, but I forgot to get a picture taken with them! Oh, well…there will be another time, and as the old Irish prayer states, "God willing," I'll see them at our next big International Convention (which will be in Toronto, Canada, at the end of June 2005.) I think of our program conventions as *family reunions* now, because *they are* part of my spiritual family.

Today, we both sponsor many people in each of our Twelve-Step programs and we live a very happy, busy life. Again, God willing, we can keep doing that for many more years. We are passing on to others who are just beginning the program that which we have been given. God keeps giving us so many blessings, if we didn't give it away to others, we'd be completely inundated with them. That would only stagnate our growth. I live my life one day at a time, and I continue to attend many meetings, sometimes even when I am very tired in the evening and have a struggle finding the energy. The rewards have been a beautiful, improved, happy new life. My program helps me use the principles of the fellowship in all of my affairs; my service work, church, my husband and family, and even with non-program friends.

I've heard it said that no one ever graduates in our spiritual Twelve-Step program. Maybe not, but we have lots of celebrations along the way. I know I'll never go back to the person I was before coming to these rooms. Between us, Paul and I have about a hundred years of relationship experiences, and we've learned a great deal from all of them that we willingly share with others now.

I have an awesome guide in my Power Greater Than Myself, who has a great road map that I follow, step by step, on my spiritual journey through life. I'm enjoying all the love and joy I'm given along the way, moment to moment. With the help of my God, I now have the inner peace I always yearned for, and even during chaos, I keep that God-given deep tranquility. I don't live in a fantasy realm today as I did before working the Steps, but my dream is that we can make a better world for ourselves—*and all others*—by using the Twelve Steps in our daily contact with each other as human beings. By changing my actions, perceptions, and perspectives, I may or may not encourage my loved ones or others I am in relationships with to change and become my ideals of how they should think and behave. They have the right to live their own lives as they see fit, guided by their own Higher Power, without any criticism, judgment, contempt, or resentments from my perspectives. Living these principles has taken me many years and a great deal of self-discipline, but the rewards of living a serene, happy life make all of my efforts worthwhile.

Today I make daily choices for my own benefit, with guidance from God and not necessarily to influence any others in their decisions that affect me. Although it is possible that my living example may lead them to consider working the Twelve Steps into his/her own way of life. It was the dream of one of the founders of my program, and also of mine, that perhaps one day the majority of people in this world will live a life based on the principles of the Twelve Spiritual Steps.

As I age, gracefully I hope, I am aware that I'm losing physical strength. If I'm active for a significant number of hours, my energy dissipates more quickly than it did in my fifties and early sixties, but I have choices and solutions today. I always felt, when I was younger, that I had to stay busy. Everything seemed to demand my immediate attention and had to be "just so." Now I give myself permission to rest whenever I feel like it. That is the true joy of being a senior for me; I can let things go until tomorrow, and that's perfectly okay now. The world won't fall apart if I indulge myself by simply listening to digital music.

No matter how old I become, I find there are still many ways to change and grow. My support groups and the spirituality of the Steps give me the strength and encouragement to keep coming back to do that, because we are united under a Greater Power that a lot of us know as God.

I continually pray, "Let there be peace on this beautiful planet Earth." I have a firm belief that if we live according to the principles in the Twelve Steps, with the management and spiritual source of wisdom from a Power Greater than any human being, we may create a better world for children today, and for all generations that follow. And I ask my God to "Let it begin with me."

With my love to each and every one, and it is my prayer that you may always find the happiness and serenity in life that a Higher Power feels we all richly deserve.

Mary-Glen Scot 2005

978-0-595-33919-
0-595-33919-0

Printed in the United States
114829LV00002B/76/A